Imperfection

Cultural Dialectics

Series editor: Raphael Foshay

The difference between subject and object slices through subject as well as through object.
—Theodor Adorno

Cultural Dialectics provides an open arena in which to debate questions of culture and dialectic — their practices, their theoretical forms, and their relations to one another and to other spheres and modes of inquiry. Approaches that draw on any of the following are especially encouraged: continental philosophy, psychoanalysis, the Frankfurt and Birmingham schools of cultural theory, deconstruction, gender theory, postcoloniality, and interdisciplinarity.

SERIES TITLES

Northern Love: An Exploration of Canadian Masculinity
  Paul Nonnekes

Making Game: An Essay on Hunting, Familiar Things,
and the Strangeness of Being Who One Is
  Peter L. Atkinson

Valences of Interdisciplinarity: Theory, Practice, Pedagogy
  Edited by Raphael Foshay

Imperfection
  Patrick Grant

IMPERFECTION

Patrick Grant

AU PRESS

Copyright © 2012 Patrick Grant
Published by AU Press, Athabasca University
1200, 10011–109 Street, Edmonton, AB T5J 3S8

ISBN 978-1-926836-75-1 (print) 978-1-926836-76-8 (PDF) 978-1-926836-77-5 (epub)
A volume in the Cultural Dialectics series
ISSN 1915-836X (print) 1915-8378 (digital)

Cover and interior design by Natalie Olsen, Kisscut Design.
Printed and bound in Canada by Marquis Book Printers.

Library and Archives Canada Cataloguing in Publication
Grant, Patrick
Imperfection / Patrick Grant.

(Cultural dialectics, 1915-836x)
Includes bibliographical references.
Issued also in electronic formats.
ISBN 978-1-926836-75-1

1. Philosophy — History. 2. Criticism. 3. Imperfection. 4. Self.
5. Philosophical theology. 6. Ethnic conflict — Religious aspects. I. Title.
II. Series: Cultural dialectics

BD450.G73 2012   128   C2012-901432-X

We acknowledge the financial support of the Government of Canada through
the Canada Book Fund (CBF) for our publishing activities.

Canada Council   Conseil des Arts
for the Arts   du Canada

Assistance provided by the Government of Alberta, Alberta Multimedia Development Fund.

Government
of Alberta ■

This book has been published with the help of a grant
from the Canadian Federation for the Humanities and
Social Sciences, through the Aid to Scholarly publications
Programme, using funds provided by the Social Sciences
and Humanities Research Council of Canada.

Canadian **Federation** for the
Humanities and Social Sciences
Fédération canadienne
des sciences humaines

Cover image: Lauri Rotko/Folio Images/Getty Images

For Larry

Imperfect and full of faults as we are,
we're never justified in stifling the ideal,
and what extends into the infinite as
if it were no concern of ours.

VINCENT VAN GOGH, May 1883

There is no excellent beauty that hath
not some strangeness in the proportion.

FRANCIS BACON, *Of Beauty*

Contents

PREFACE   xi

INTRODUCTION   I

——————————————————— PART I *Imperfection*

1   Plato and the Limits of Idealism   9

2   The Van Gogh Letters: The Art of the Unfinished   17

3   The Trouble with Visions   31

4   Northern Ireland, Sri Lanka, and Regressive Inversion   41

5   Osama, Theo, and the Burnt Fool's Bandaged Finger   49

6   What the Buddha Didn't Say   57

7   Not So Good News: The Gospel According to Mark   67

——————————————————— PART II *Self*

8   Immortal Souls and State Executions   79

9   The Eyes Have It: Seeing One's Self and Others   89

10 The God of Battles and the Irish Dimension of   99
    Shakespeare's *Henry V*

11 Crucifying Harry: Victims, Scapegoats, and the Northern   107
    Ireland Troubles

12 Talking to the Cyclops: On Violence and Self-Destruction   115

13 Doing Nothing About It: Taoism, Selflessness, and   121
    Non-Action

14 Cliff Jumpers and Delta Dwellers: On Religious Language   133
    and Commitment

PART III *Freedom*

15   Dr. Johnson, Freedom, and the Book of Psalms   143

16   Sex, Society, and *Romeo and Juliet*   155

17   Cartoons from Denmark and the March of the Zombies   165

18   Vergil and the Almighty Dollar   173

19   Endgame in Sri Lanka: Dharmapala's Legacy and   183
     Rajapaksa's War

20   Jung and *The Secret of the Golden Flower*   195

21   Kieslowski's *Red:* Fraternity in the Making   205

BIBLIOGRAPHICAL NOTES   225

Preface

This book has developed partly from a retrospective view of other books I have happened to write over the course of an academic career. On the face of it, these books are an eclectic mix, beginning with studies of Renaissance English literature and proceeding by way of inquiries into the scientific revolution, Christian mysticism, literary modernism, the New Testament, the idea of the person, ethnic conflict in Northern Ireland, and Buddhism in Sri Lanka. Although I was aware that these projects were interconnected, I would have been hard pressed to set out explicitly the key values that were (more or less) tacitly at work in the project as a whole. In the following chapters, I revisit several questions raised by these earlier studies, but I do so mainly to clarify what I take to be the key guiding principles and ideas that have been at work throughout and which in turn underpin a certain view, or assessment, of the human predicament that, for better or worse, we find ourselves sharing.

In a nutshell, this view, or assessment, can be summarized by the observation that people are imperfect but they have ideas about perfection, and the most interesting and creative things that people do are produced from within this opposition between the ideal and the actual. In itself, this claim is straightforward, but its implications are less so, and are explored in a series of essay-like chapters which have a bearing especially on the present state of the God debate, on modern ethnic conflicts in which religion is a marker of identity, and on the idea of freedom in relation to the uncertainties of personal identity and self-determination.

Acknowledgements should go all the way back, but the list would be all but endless. Nonetheless, I would like to single out one particular lodestar that has been there from the beginning. From the first undergraduate essay almost exactly a half-century ago, down to the present volume, Laurence Lerner has, with unfailing goodwill and almost terrifying endurance, been engaged, vigorous, testing, humane, insightful, and difficult to please. It has been a long conversation; I am the better for it, and, with gratitude, I look forward to keeping it going.

Earlier versions of chapters 5, 10, 11, 12, and 14 appeared in *Fortnight* magazine in February 2005 (no. 433), December 2003 (no. 420), October 2004 (no. 429), December 2002 (no. 409), and September 2004 (no. 415). Chapter 9 draws on materials published in *Personalism and the Politics of Culture* (London: Macmillan, 1996), chap. 4; the remarks on Dharmapala in chapter 19 draw on materials published in *Buddhism and Ethnic Conflict in Sri Lanka* (New York: State University of New York Press, 2009), chap. 4.

"Only madmen and fools are pleased with themselves: no wise man is good enough for his own satisfaction." I'm not sure that I entirely agree with this statement by the seventeenth-century philosopher-theologian Benjamin Whichcote, but he puts his finger on a fact about human experience with which I am mainly concerned in the following pages. That is, human beings are distinctive among the creatures because humans can conceive of and aspire to a perfect or ideal good even though they themselves remain imperfect. Whichcote's wise man understands this and accepts the disparity. By contrast, the madmen and fools suffer from a deluded self-satisfaction that, we can assume, might make them dangerous.

As Whichcote's aphorism suggests, ideas about perfection and about the self are closely bound up with one another. That is, the notion that we are autonomous moral agents develops alongside our acceptance of ideals. Thus, an individual who is committed to a moral ideal and who fails to live up to it is likely to experience guilt and feel irresponsible. For such a person, the enduring identity of the self over time as the bearer of responsibilities is assumed as self-evident.

Whichcote doesn't mention whether or not guilt and responsibility accompany the wise man's dissatisfaction with himself, but instead he warns against what for him is a bigger problem: the madness and folly of those who don't feel dissatisfaction at all because they are sufficiently good already. One step further and we find the madmen and fools entertaining delusions of grandeur — the idea that they are perfect already and can treat others accordingly, playing God.

Historically, religion has done much to explain and manage relationships between the self and the ideas about perfection to which it aspires and by which it is simultaneously shaped and rebuked. Especially in the main monotheistic traditions emergent from the Middle East, God, who alone is perfect, creates and oversees the human drama, and religion focuses on human experiences of imperfection, responsibility, guilt, and aspiration — experiences within which the sense of individual, autonomous personhood is shaped. But during the past century, globalization has rapidly made accessible the diversity and sophistication of other world religions, and (at least in some quarters) secularism has enabled a powerful critique of the truth claims of religion in general.

For instance, the recent flurry of attacks on religion, largely in response to dangerous kinds of fundamentalism emergent especially from the Abrahamic faith traditions, East and West, has given short shrift to the explanatory power of religion in enabling any humane understanding at all of the "wretched creature who can apprehend perfection," as T.E. Hulme says (reproducing Whichcote's idea, but with an additional acerbic edge). Certainly, the strenuous atheism of the recent anti-religious vanguard is welcome at least for its insistence on the right of unbelief and its attack on the follies, cruelties, and superstitions that can and ought to be laid at religion's door. And the polemicists are right: the fact is, we don't know what happens after we die, we don't know why we or the universe are here, and the mystery of existence remains as impenetrable as it is self-evident. If asserting such things makes me an atheist along with those others, then I am pleased to be one.

Yet for a Buddhist (the many varieties of Buddhism notwithstanding) these assertions would not be as troubling as they are for many, perhaps most, Christians. Buddhism is sometimes described as atheist, though in fact the Buddha — in the Pali Canon, for instance — neither affirms nor denies God's existence. It is not an important question for him, and he feels that without having to bother about it we can attend better to the suffering world around us. For the Buddha, the mystery of origins remains just that, a mystery. Life in the present is sufficient, and is affirmed by the attempt to liberate ourselves and others from suffering. Also, corresponding to this lack of concern about a creator God, Buddhism has a highly provisional sense of the self. Individual selfhood is a loose aggregate of feelings, thoughts, sensations, memories, and is not a substantive unity. Perfection consists in being liberated not only from suffering but also from the self, and we are responsible for the patient work of bringing this about, discarding our illusions in the process.

Still, perhaps surprisingly, Buddhist non-theism is less exclusive of, say, Jesus's preaching about the Kingdom of Heaven than we might at first think. The Cross also is a protest against suffering in the world, and liberation depends on us understanding its critical force, for if we don't treat our neighbour justly in the here and now we don't love God. Even such an arcane doctrine as the Trinity can make sense in this context, if understood from the perspective of philosophical theology. That is, God the Father represents the unfathomable mystery of origins; the Son is the mediator of that mystery specifically to us humans; the Spirit is the keeping alive of the Son's historical mission. These three elements are interdependent and cannot be adequately understood separately. To unbelievers, the Trinity can easily seem a nonsense, but some co-operation with its symbolic language can discover how it addresses the irreducible mystery of origins and the tragedy of suffering with which people contend throughout history, seeking to realize the joy of life within the harmonious interrelationship of community (the three persons as one).

Christianity and Buddhism are therefore not so far apart in how they attempt to involve believers in immediate and practical ways in the quest for liberation, an ideal in contrast to which the problem of imperfection — that is, suffering and injustice — is itself discovered and confronted. In this quest, Jesus and the Buddha agree that mere self-concern (egotism, selfishness, and the like) is an impediment to the freedom we seek. Transcendence of the ego and ego-inflation are opposites — just as are heaven and hell, sanctity and megalomania, community and tyranny. There is no disputing that in the history of religions, the megalomania-hell-tyranny trinity has often trumped sanctity-community-heaven. But many believers understand this without losing faith in religion's better side, and on the reverse of the coin, there are plenty of megalomaniac, infernal secularists about as well.

In short, religions are human constructs, and their fundamental metaphysical assertions are a symbolic reckoning of our human predicament, wherein we find ourselves confronted by the scandal of suffering and imperfection while aspiring nonetheless to ideals marked by the absence of such things. But religious people don't know any more than the rest of us about the overarching mysteries of existence and consciousness. Nor does it help to conflate religions (as I have just been doing with Buddhism and Christianity) to a degree that obscures their differences. Nonetheless, for many practical and moral purposes, complex allegiances do exist beyond the lines drawn by dogma, and there is a broad spectrum of understanding and commitment among the religions themselves. Dogma alone doesn't tell us anything about the spirit in which it is understood, or whether or not it is a vehicle for promoting justice and compassion. As the theologian Jürgen Moltmann says, the problem of suffering (imperfection) cannot be answered, nor can righteous-ness (the ideal) be surrendered. That is the basic contradiction within which the *humanum,* the human thing itself, is shaped, and careful discernment is required to untangle the truth claims of religion and of other kinds of discourse without oversimplifying how they engage the core contradiction Moltmann describes.

All of which brings me back to the idea with which I began, namely that aspirations to perfection awaken us to our actual imper-fection. Some implications of this idea can now be stated in the form of a small number of assertions, as follows.

A sense of the self as an autonomous agent and the bearer of responsibilities develops in the gap between people's actual imper-fections and the ideals to which they aspire. The notion that we have a single, unitary self is yet another ideal that we do not (and cannot) live up to; rather, personal identity is provisional, emerging from the body's inarticulate skills and preconscious knowing. A sufficiently stable sense of self can be nurtured within the family and its exten-sions (clan, tribe, nation), but conflicts perennially arise between passionate group (family) loyalties and an individual's adherence to a transcendent principle or idea. Such conflicts are central to how autonomous moral agency is discovered, through which, in turn, a community might be freely shaped in contradistinction to the con-straints of group loyalties and obligations. Freedom in this sense entails some degree of individual responsibility, but (if it exists at all) freedom is limited, and it is useful to acknowledge this as a way of avoiding the twin perils of ego-inflation and self-hatred. Finally, the right to unbelief should be valued and defended, not least because principled secular unbelief shows that people don't have to be reli-gious to be moral, and in so doing encourages religious people to behave morally as an affirmation that their religious claims are, at least, not egregiously harmful.

My title, *Imperfection,* addresses this set of concerns, and the book is divided into three main sections reflecting the main topics I have outlined above: imperfection, the self, and freedom. I do not so much present a systematic argument as a set of interlinked sorties, as it were ("essais" in the basic sense), each pertaining to the topic in hand. Also, I attempt to address the book to non-specialized readers and to avoid as much as possible the formal apparatus of academic discourse. Each chapter can be read independently, and there is no special reason to proceed sequentially (browsers are welcome). For those who might prefer to read straight through, the sections and chapters are interconnected in ways that I describe as the argument proceeds.

PART I *Imperfection*

I

Plato and the Limits of Idealism

It makes good sense to start with Plato (428–348 BCE), the first Western philosopher whose writings survive in more than fragmentary form, and at the heart of whose thinking is a preoccupation with the fact that ideas are real and perfect in a way that material things are not. In short, Plato is the first Idealist, and his thinking is usually described in a manner that focuses on this point. Yet Plato's *Dialogues* are bewilderingly complex and all-but-endlessly engaging, not least because his idealism led him simultaneously to discover the pervasiveness and significance of human imperfection, and that suffering and injustice are problems that the salve of reason does not entirely cure. Plato's most enduring achievement remains in how he wrestles with this set of issues, but to provide some further sense of how he discovered them in the first place, let us turn briefly to his predecessors in ancient Greece during the sixth and fifth centuries BCE.

Like all geniuses, Plato chose the right time to be born — a time, that is, when his extraordinary talents were fitted to produce a new understanding of ideas explored, but not consolidated, by a wide range of earlier thinkers. These early philosophers had struggled to understand the world as Homer described it in the fabulous, brightly contoured narratives of his great epics, the *Iliad* and the *Odyssey*. That is, the philosophers wanted to learn about the principles by which Homer's gods kept order in the cosmos, given that the gods behaved erratically and were often at odds with one another. Likewise, the philosophers wanted to know what principles could best regulate human behaviour, which was itself as changeable as the cosmos and the gods and, as Homer shows, is frequently influenced by both.

Thales, Anaximander, Anaximines, Heraclitus, Parmenides, Empedocles, Democritus, and the Pythagoreans offered explanations focused on the cosmic aspects of the question, speculating about laws and principles that provide stability in a constantly shifting material world. Plato's great teacher, Socrates, began also by seeking to understand change in nature, but, like his main antagonists, the Sophists, he decided to switch his attention to the changeableness of human behaviour. That is, Socrates wanted to know what principles should guide us so that we might better bring to order our frequent unruliness and moral confusion.

Instructed by his predecessors, Plato sought to investigate both of these large issues and to understand the ordered dance of the heavenly bodies as well as the moral behaviour of human beings. Moreover, he thought that the answer to the first question (prompted by the cosmological theorists) would be the same kind of answer as would explain the second (prompted by Socrates). What holds for the universe at large holds for ourselves within the universe, and also for the good society should we be able to construct it. In short, Plato believed in the inherent rationality of the cosmos, and in our minds being so ordered as to mirror and understand its workings. For this reason, he is usually described as an idealist. That is, he is convinced that ideas are real because they don't change, and he believed that reason gives reliable access to the unchanging laws that govern the universe, including the moral behaviour of human beings.

In short, Plato happened along when the time was ripe for gathering and sorting the rich harvest of poetry, philosophy, and ethical and political theory that had been produced so abundantly by the remarkable phase of Greek culture directly preceding him. He would make a banquet out of this abundance, transforming, rearranging, and re-presenting it by way of his own personal alchemy, leaving us with his great collection, the *Dialogues*. Yet he does not provide us with a clearly worked-out system, and his dialogues are more like a smorgasbord than a formal banquet. Everything is there, but it can be confusing to know where to begin, and, when you have had enough, how exactly to describe what you have taken in. Although the idealizing thrust of Plato's main arguments remains clear, he is everywhere aware also of the resistance offered to his theories by the sheer, confusing weight of experience. Why, for instance, do people so often act in ways that flagrantly contradict what their reason clearly tells them is best to do?

When Plato wrote, the laws of logic had not been formulated, and Socrates (Plato's spokesman, more or less, throughout the *Dialogues*) frequently argues by way of dubious analogies, fanciful correspondences, and tendentious assertions — "Plato's ravings," as David Hume said, in mild exasperation. Indeed, a first-time reader is likely to feel more than a little perplexed by the often peculiar, dilatory arguments offered by Socrates and by the galaxy of characters who debate with him. It all has a strangely dazing effect, as if one were entering into a mental state uncertainly poised between sleeping and waking. Philosophy, we feel, is struggling to come into its own domain, and an open, flexible, and even confusing exchange of ideas is necessary for this to happen. But Plato had also arrived at the highly significant understanding that you can't conduct a philosophical discussion with just anybody. Socrates, after all, had been put to death by authorities who thought that his teachings threatened their traditional values. They were unwilling to examine the issues with him philosophically, and

Socrates's death confirms how customary practice and reasoned argument can be at odds. Independent thinking, it seems, is a skill that has to be cultivated by a patient process of education which entails a new way of understanding, a willingness to examine ideas on their own merit, without regard for received religious and moral traditions. The disposition required to argue well is therefore as important as the ideas themselves and underpins the very enterprise of philosophy, contending as it does with cultural prejudice, un-self-critical thinking, and plain irrationality. We can see something of how this is so in Plato's most famous dialogue, the *Republic*.

In the *Republic,* Plato sets out to describe the ideal state, but in many respects what he comes up with will strike us as a good deal less than ideal. Non-Greeks can be enslaved; war is accepted as a permanent condition; there is a eugenic program to ensure the propagation of an elite caste; order is maintained according to oppressively hierarchical principles. Yet, as the dialogue proceeds, we can see that Plato himself comes increasingly to realize that his own theories are removing him too far from the world of actual experience. At one point, Socrates is asked outright whether or not the ideal republic is "a practical possibility" (231), and this is what he says:

> Then we were looking for an ideal when we tried to define justice and injustice, and to describe what the perfectly just or perfectly unjust man would be like if he ever existed. By looking at these perfect patterns and the measure of happiness or unhappiness they would enjoy, we force ourselves to admit that the nearer we approximate to them the more nearly we share their lot. That was our purpose, rather than to show that they could be realized in practice, was it not? (232)

Socrates admits that he is in pursuit of an "ideal" and wants to describe "perfect patterns." But he also suggests that there might not be a "perfectly just" man ("if he ever existed" suggests that the ideal might not be attainable). Nonetheless, the effort to "approximate" the ideal is the important thing, rather than showing that the ideal "could be realized in practice."

This is not the only place where Socrates makes a concession, acknowledging that experience resists the "perfect patterns" prescribed by reason. A further example occurs in the mythopoetic passage with which the *Republic* ends. This is a story told by Er, "son of Armenius, a native of Pamphylia" (394). By giving the last word to a non-Greek, Plato indicates that the discourse has now left the realm of philosophy (Greeks can do philosophy; outsiders can't). Er is said to have died in battle but was revived and was able to tell "what he had seen in the other world" (394). Mainly, he assures us that we will be judged according to how well or badly we have lived, and his account of the afterlife incorporates a grand cosmic myth, the main purpose of which is to confirm that, outside the boundaries of our limited experience, justice will be done in a manner that confirms the rational structure of the cosmos itself. Because Socrates has not been able to demonstrate that a rationally ordered, perfect society could in fact exist on earth, Plato gives us this concluding myth, urging us to hope that everything will in the end work out for the best. Argument alone cannot bring us all the way to this conclusion, and so philosophy at last yields to poetry.

All of which helps to explain why poetry gives Plato, the philosopher, so much trouble. At the start of the *Republic* he denounces Homer's representations of the gods, pointing out that these supposedly superior divine powers often behave disgracefully and unjustly. He worries also about the corruptive effect of poetry and mythology on children, and he evicts poets from the ideal state, except for those who might offer acceptable hymns of praise. In the second half of the dialogue he attacks poetry again, this time as a poor imitator of reality and as a dangerous inflamer of unruly emotion at the expense of reason.

And yet, although he censors the poets, Plato himself cannot shake poetry off, and throughout the *Republic* his own most compelling passages are themselves often poetic, as in the complex, interwoven allegories of the sun, line, and cave with which, at the very heart of the dialogue, he attempts to describe the (indescribable) Absolute Good. Then, at last, as we see, he gives us the myth of Er, inviting us to aspire to a perfect justice, an outcome pleasing to reason even if beyond the horizons of our damaged history.

Throughout the *Republic,* then, Plato struggles to discover and acknowledge the limitations of reason, even as he does his utmost to promote reason's cause. In this context, Thrasymachus is a centrally important character, even though he leaves the conversation early. Plato introduces Thrasymachus after some brief, opening exchanges between Socrates, the old man Cephalus, and his son Polymarchus. Socrates has an easy time, and these characters are readily manipulated. We might even feel some relief when Thrasymachus, a trained Sophist, declares that he is having no more of Socrates's sleights of hand. Thrasymachus breaks in rudely and attacks Socrates for being a sham (64). He then offers his own view of justice, which he defines as "what is in the interest of the stronger party." There is no appeal to ideals here, just an assertion, a full-frontal embrace of "tyranny," which Thrasymachus defines as "wholesale plunder, sacred or profane, private or public" (73).

The exchange with the angry, forceful Thrasymachus continues at some length, and when Socrates at last begins to gain an advantage, Thrasymachus responds by bluntly refusing to accept the conclusions. And here Socrates encounters one important limitation of philosophy's power to persuade: you cannot reason with people who are convinced that reasoning itself is futile, because, when all the talk is done, might is still right. Terrorists, psychopathic sadists, tyrants, and louts everywhere at some point simply cancel the philosopher's guiding principle: let's talk about it. Thrasymachus is their exemplar, and if philosophical discussion is to continue, he must leave, as he does.

Then a remarkable thing happens. Two other characters, Glaucon and Adeimantus, take up where Thrasymachus left off. Glaucon provides a summary of Thrasymachus's main argument, offering to continue with it even though assuring Socrates, "I don't believe all this myself" (89). Although Thrasymachus leaves the discussion (later, it is indicated that he continues to hang around, observing), the force of his objections remains. Throughout the *Republic*, discussions about tyranny and the rule of force keep bringing us back to the "Thrasymachus factor," and Thrasymachus remains as a sort of philosophical Cyclops, a menacing reminder that reason itself can be used to argue for the futility of reason. One name for this position is nihilism, which, in the end, Socrates realizes he can't defeat. And so Plato concludes with a myth about perfect justice, hoping to keep alive, at least, our aspiration to the ideal.

But why do Glaucon and Adeimantus insist on putting a case in which they say they don't believe? As we see, it isn't possible to enter into dialogue with just anyone, and the argument with Thrasymachus breaks down because he won't seriously consider positions other than those he already holds. When pressed, he resorts to a disagreeable attitude in order to short-circuit further discussion. But when Glaucon and Adeimantus continue to make Thrasymachus's case, they bring a different attitude to bear, sharing with Socrates a willingness to discover where the argument leads. The ability to carry on a discussion in such a spirit is the central skill on which philosophy itself depends, and in a remarkable letter, Plato explains how this is so.

The study of virtue and vice, Plato says in Letter 7, "must be carried on by constant practice throughout a long period." Then, after a suitable amount of "benevolent disputation by the use of question and answer without jealousy, at last in a flash understanding of each blazes up, and the mind, as it exerts all its power to the limit of human capacity, is flooded with light." Although insight might occur in a flash, it is engendered patiently by people who have learned how to argue with a respect for evidence and for alternative, soundly reasoned positions. Admittedly, within the *Dialogues*, Socrates himself is not always decorous or respectful, as when he bamboozles a variety of dupes who have the temerity to take him on. But the historical Socrates died for the right to go on asking uncomfortable questions and to go on encouraging young people in the art of disputation. Plato knew the value of what Socrates taught and died for, and he knew that a sure sign of tyranny is the refusal of the right to answer back, to say anything more, to voice dissent, to keep open the discussion.

In the *Republic,* Thrasymachus assumes various guises, as he does throughout human history, but his final argument is always the same: he will stop your mouth by force. Although Socrates can't altogether get the better of Thrasymachus, neither does he fail to confront him. The twists and turns of Socrates's arguments, ruses, flights of fancy, strained analogies, doubtful and peculiar deductions serve at least to keep the key questions alive, and also, by implication, they are ranged against the silencing of dissent. In comparison, Plato's more explicit thinking about a perfect, transcendent world of Forms and an unrealizable (and unlivable) ideal state, remains, as it should, open for discussion. But the more interesting dimension of the *Republic* remains in how Plato presents the conflict between the ideals to which he invites us to aspire as a matter of personal responsibility and the daunting realization of the intractability of injustice to which the idealism itself awakens us.

2

The Van Gogh Letters
The Art of the Unfinished

The idea of beauty has drawn the attention of philosophers from ancient times. Plato, whose *Republic* we have been considering in the previous chapter, has a good deal to say about the formal perfection of the ideally beautiful. But another, un-Platonic, aspect of beauty is emphasized, for instance, by the seventeenth-century philosopher Francis Bacon, when he says, "There is no excellent beauty that hath not some strangeness in the proportion." That is, the most beautiful things have some degree of asymmetry or imperfection which, somehow, makes beauty itself more poignant and affecting.

To consider this point further, let us turn to a painter who was preoccupied with unconventional kinds of beauty and who has left a larger collection of personal reflections on this topic than has any other major graphic artist. In his voluminous letters, Vincent Van Gogh repeatedly distinguishes between real beauty and the merely decorative and conventionally harmonious. In so doing, he explores the subtle interconnection between beauty and imperfection, and for Van Gogh, this exploration established a further connection between painting and morality. Not surprisingly in this light, there are close ties between the reception of Van Gogh's paintings and the story of how he lived his own difficult — in the end, tragic — life.

Try visiting the Van Gogh Museum in Amsterdam any day, any time, any season, and you find it full of people — a perpetual spate, all ages, nationalities, conditions. You might feel, even, that you are somehow among pilgrims — the museum become, as it were, a secular shrine. This is because, by and large, visitors are drawn not just by the paintings but also by the man who painted them. Ask a random sample about their reasons for coming and most will tell you something about Vincent's life. Homage to the man and admiration of his art are all but inseparable here. The museum shop, which offers fine reproductions and high-quality books, also sells box-loads of Vincent-themed mementos worthy of Lourdes.

Vincent himself would have been of two minds about all this. On the one hand, he insisted that in literature and painting the main thing is to find the artist, and he cites Zola with approval: "In the painting (the work of art), I look for, I love the man — the artist" (515). Certainly, in his own paintings he meets us everywhere with a discomposing personal directness, making an intimate claim on us, at times not entirely comfortable. And so he would have liked the fact that a sea of people from across the globe have kept coming to commune with him, the artist, and he would also have liked the fact that so many of his works are displayed in one place. He often insisted on the importance of seeing his work together, not piecemeal, because he thought that a collection allows better access to the man himself.

On the other hand, academicism and official museum culture frequently irritated Vincent, though he allowed that good critical writing could be artistic (854) and he visited museums, often enthusiastically. Also, he despised fame. Borrowing from Carlyle, he compared an artist who had gained celebrity to a glow-worm pinned to a lady's hat (660), and, elsewhere, he says that fame is like putting the lit end of a cigar into your mouth (673). Still (never shy of contradiction), he hoped that some of his work would have lasting value (604), and he spent a good deal of time and effort trying to make the Impressionists famous enough to sell for better prices (588), thereby boosting his brother Theo's income as an art dealer and securing his own stipend, dutifully sent by Theo but sometimes precarious.

In short, Vincent wouldn't have wanted the fame for its own sake. But he would have welcomed the people, especially those who might find consolation in what his paintings have to say to them — those astonishing, silent voices through which we meet him, so various and yet so insistently, so recognizably himself.

Throughout the museum, the better-known facts about Vincent's life are presented in easily readable, large-print banners positioned strategically among the paintings. The intensity of his dedication, the integrity of his vision, the physical and mental anguish that caused him to be hospitalized, the fierce affirmation of life from the heart of disappointment and tragedy, the extraordinary courage, and his tragic death at age thirty-seven — these are parts of a story which most visitors know at least in outline before they arrive.

But how famous would the paintings be if the biographical facts were unavailable? We can never know for sure, but there is little risk in assuming that their genius would be recognized for what it is, as Vincent's distinguished contemporaries — Monet, Pissarro, and Gauguin among them — saw from the start. Everywhere, his pictures come at us with a distinctive, surging energy, a forcefulness revealing also a surprisingly refined sympathy, evoked in us as we recognize how poignantly it is expressed by him. He had discovered in a highly personal manner how line and colour communicate independently of what is represented, yet always, for him, without losing contact with ordinary, recognizable objects. One result is that through his paintings our common world discloses to us something of our innermost hopes, desires, fears, and longings, discovered and shared in and through everyday things and people depicted, as Vincent never tired of saying, with "a certain life" (528) or "*power of expression*" (439). He explains how he sought deliberately to simplify and exaggerate in order to reveal what he called the "essence" (336) of a thing — the place where, in its depths, it responds to and mirrors the human concerns of the observer. His fierce impasto, seething contours, and breakneck speed of production are governed by these aims. One result is that his technique can often seem untutored, whereas in fact it is the result of an intense and rigorous apprenticeship. Thus, he explains how he worked painstakingly to develop his technique to a point where people will "swear by all that's holy that we have no technique" (439). Clearly, this is risky — daring, even challenging, the viewer to trust — and one result is that Vincent can be a polarizing figure in his work, as he was in his life. Yet once you allow yourself to see things his way, the results are breathtaking.

Again pressing us, Vincent insists also on finding beauty in the ignored and rejected — in poor people, peasants, miners, prostitutes, the world-weary, the conventionally ugly. In choosing such subjects, he wants his pictures to offer a consolation which is also a protest against suffering, degradation, rejection. "And in painting I'd like to say something consoling," he says, and "to paint men or women with that *je ne sais quoi* of the eternal, of which the halo used to be the symbol" (673). This sanctification of the ordinary extends also to his landscapes, which he sees as evoking and mirroring our human concerns. "If I were to make landscapes," he tells Theo, "there would always be something of the figure about them" (212), and he cites with approval a remark by Israels about a landscape by Dupré: "It's just like a painting of a figure" (483). Indeed, Vincent's depiction of any object at all is never a mere reproduction of appearances, and he thought it a waste of time to seek after such an effect. Rather, young corn "evokes an emotion like that aroused by the expression of a sleeping child," and "the grass trodden down at the side of a road looks tired and dusty like the inhabitants of a poor quarter" (292). He likes to paint old, gnarled trees that produce ethereal new blossom — as hope and beauty might spring even from hard and bitter experience. His famous sunflowers are radiant and heavy with "gratitude" (853) as he says, turning their great, laden heads faithfully to the source of life. In everything he painted he sought this kind of expressive power, reaching out for our recognition and sympathetic, reciprocal gaze, our willingness to celebrate the natural miracle of existence despite suffering and injustice. "Sorrowful yet always rejoicing," he liked to say, especially in his earlier letters, but he never ceased confirming this truth to which the apostle Paul had first directed him.

The greatness of the paintings is (at least) in some such achievement, some such combination of qualities. They confront us and also embrace us; they present a rough, unruly challenge but extend also an unguarded compassion. And when we see them together, we cannot miss the integrity of the vision and the courage informing Vincent's persistent, unorthodox exploration of the means of its expression. Visitors would come, yes, just for the paintings, and so they should. Yet there is something even grander and more impressive when we see how Vincent attempted to live and write as he painted, and how the integrity and nobility of his admittedly difficult character inform the paintings and yet are not confined by them.

And so we return to the fact that not just the special paintings draw the visitors, but also the special man. In turn, we know as much as we do about the man because we have so much of his correspondence — 902 letters survive, extending from 1872, when he was nineteen years old, to his death in 1890, at age thirty-seven. Of these, 819 were written by Vincent, at first in Dutch and then, later, in French (a couple are in English), and some 83 others are addressed to him. There are approximately 3,800 pages, a fraction of what he probably wrote, but a substantial collection nonetheless. The majority (658) are written to Theo, and most of the others are written to the painters Anthon Van Rappard, Émile Bernard, and Paul Gauguin. Twenty-one are addressed to his sister, Willemien ("Wil"), and he writes occasionally to a further assortment of people.

Dating is a problem (for the most part, Vincent didn't bother), and tone and register are often gauged to fit the recipient. He is solicitous and kindly to Wil, racey and unbuttoned with Bernard, academic and theoretical with Van Rappard, and with Theo he expresses a spectrum of emotions of Dostoevskian range and variety. Not surprisingly, his opinions change and develop. For instance, his enthusiasm for Bunyan and Thomas à Kempis yields to Balzac and Zola as he becomes committed to painting rather than religion. Also, his writing is shot through with ambivalence and conflict. Thus, adulation of his father yields to bitter reproof and denunciation, then guiltily reverts to respect and affection, the whole difficult matter never finally resolved. His gratitude for Theo's support is not proof against his apprehension that Theo's money might cease coming, and Vincent can be distastefully manipulative or unctuously grateful by turns, as well as touchingly appreciative of his brother's generosity. The disastrous love relationships with Kee Vos, Sien Hoornik, and Margot Begemann are painful in the extreme, an apt preface to his fraught relationship with Paul Gauguin, which ended, famously, with Vincent cutting off a piece of his own ear and being confined in a mental hospital. In short, the letters are full of incident, and a reader who goes all the way through will likely have to put them down now and then and walk about, breathing deeply.

Yet for the most part the letters are not so dramatic. At one point, Vincent confides that he might have become "a thinker" (405) — an academic, perhaps a theologian like his admired uncle Stricker — and elsewhere he suggests that he could have made a living as a writer (710). Even a brief sortie into the letters makes clear that he is not being fanciful about these aspirations. He reads widely, with insightful intelligence and furious energy, returning repeatedly to his favourites (Shakespeare, Dickens, Zola, Balzac, Hugo). His letters are often a way of dealing with the fact that he lacked adequately stimulating conversation, and often they are a forum for setting out his leading ideas, expressed with the same muscular force and intelligence as we find in his paintings. He has a talent for graphic description, and he provides vivid descriptions of landscapes, weather, and people, as well as of paintings, engravings, and prints. On the reflective side, he can formulate opinions with a gnomic density that arrests a reader's attention independently of context: "I'd rather paint people's eyes than cathedrals, for there's something in the eyes that isn't in the cathedral" (549); "My dear chap, never resign yourself and never be disappointed, that's the best advice I could give you" (184); "Very fine pens, like very elegant people, are sometimes amazingly impractical" (325); "The true pain and tension of creating begins at the point where you let go of the description" (244); "Even if our mind is sometimes occupied by the question *is there a God* or *does He not exist*, this is no reason for us deliberately to commit a godless act, is it?" (405).

There are countless examples of this kind of thing — perceptions unwaveringly stated, yet vibrating with implications causing us to pause to take their measure. Here, as everywhere throughout these richly varied documents, we feel the impress of a particular sensibility, the same combination of strength and liveliness we encounter in the paintings. It does not take long for a reader to realize that these letters have real literary distinction. Reading them all the way through leaves one shaken, energized, wondering — somehow enhanced in one's view of the world — in the same way as one might feel after reading a great novel. To reverse the point I made earlier, if the letters had survived and the paintings had been lost, Vincent would still have readers.

To provide some further understanding of the strength Vincent's writing, as well as the inter-involvement between his writing and his painting, I want to return to his explanation that he sought to simplify and exaggerate in order to reveal what he called the essence of a thing. As I have noticed, in this process, he never surrendered completely to abstraction (though sometimes he came close), but, rather, he depicted his own version of a recognizable, common world. Nonetheless, the exact reproduction of appearances seemed merely an academic exercise without life or real human interest, and he scolds his academically trained painter friend Anthon Van Rappard accordingly: "You have, in my opinion, a mistress [the academy] who freezes you, petrifies you and sucks your blood" (184). "My sympathies," he explains, "in the literary as well as the artistic sphere are drawn more strongly to those artists in whom I see the soul most at work." This entails "something very different from the masterly rendering of fabrics" and has, instead, "the power to invigorate" (332).

Vincent is not philosophically scrupulous when he discusses this "power to invigorate," as he does frequently, coming at the question from many angles and by way of various comparisons and analogies. But, throughout, he keeps returning to the key idea that simplification and exaggeration are basic strategies for attaining the "something very different" which brings art to life. "Simplifying the figures is something that very much preoccupies me," he writes, going on to say how he attempts to express "the whole manner" of a figure, rather than the exact features (361). He praises Van Rappard for attempting to paint like Corot by giving "only the intimate and the essential" (439), and explains how, in really getting to know and feel a subject, "I even do *my best* NOT *to give* ANY *details*" (437). "I must do more figure work" he tells Theo: "It's the study of the figure that teaches one to grasp the essential and to simplify" (805). Just a few lines before, Vincent has described two landscapes, stating that they "are exaggerations from the point of view of the arrangement, their lines are contorted like those of the ancient woodcuts" (805), and he explains how, in a self-portrait, he has focused on "exaggerating my personality" (695). He describes paintings such as the "Sower" and "Night Café" as "exaggerated" and also as seeming "atrociously ugly and bad"; yet these are "the only ones that seem to me to have a more important meaning" (680). When he turns a preliminary study into a picture, he does so "by enlarging, by simplifying"; also, "I exaggerate," but, nonetheless, "I don't invent the whole painting," which is "ready-made — but to be untangled — in the real world" (698). Again he laments that the results might be "ugly," but simplification and exaggeration remain central to his pursuit of the truth that painting can best reveal.

Always astute, Theo puts his finger on the key point: "If there are people who occupy themselves seeking the symbol by dint of torturing the form, I find it in many of your canvasses through the expression of the summary of your thoughts on nature and living beings, which you feel are so strongly attached to it. But how hard your mind must have worked and how you endangered yourself to the extreme point where vertigo is inevitable" (781). As Theo says, Vincent deliberately tortures the form to have it disclose a human significance not evident in surface appearances alone, yet inherent in them insofar as they have the potential to reveal such a significance in response to the intelligent commitment of the artist's interrogating, passionate eye.

As these examples show, simplification and exaggeration constitute a deliberate departure from the reproduction of the actual appearance of things, and to that extent Vincent means us to see that the objects he paints are represented imperfectly, both in form and colour. The perspective is all wrong in that scene with the trees, and this sky wouldn't actually have been green, and so on. Yet Vincent also insists that imperfection can be a means of realizing a truth that is especially compelling when it succeeds in incorporating the imperfection itself as part of its meaning.

Admittedly, this again is risky — part of what Theo must have meant in noticing that Vincent "endangered himself to the extreme point." Not everyone was (or is) convinced, and Vincent has always had his detractors. For what would the difference be between a merely unfinished piece of bad painting and the ecstatically true thing that a painting might be if we could only see its imperfections as integral to its expressive power? Vincent's answer to this is a series of pointers rather than a developed theoretical explanation, and he uses words such as "mysterious" (534), "essence" (336), "the power to invigorate" (332) to indicate the difference between genius and mere incompetence in the matter. Especially, he praises his favourite, Rembrandt, "magician of magicians" (550), for using the unfinished, the incompletely represented, to give depth, vividness, and dramatic power to his painting.

Vincent held that his own "inaccuracies" as he calls them, also produce an effect "truer than the literal truth" (515), and we might ask how this could be so. Part of the answer is that the artfully imperfect awakens longing — the desire for an elusive completeness. The truly beautiful is always accompanied by an undercurrent of nostalgia because beauty that is not just sentimental points beyond itself towards a longed-for fulfillment that we cannot completely have or hold, just as beauty itself is transient — which is why beautiful things can make people cry. As Vincent says, "it's neither the best paintings nor the best people — in which there are no errors or bias" (465), but a spontaneous reaching across and through our personal defects as well as the limitations of the medium of communication requires an honesty that in turn can impart a sense of vital presence.

It was a revelation for Vincent to discover how the old Dutch masters "just put it straight down" without much retouching (535), and he refers often to his own speed of execution, of setting things down "*in one go*" (537) as a way of communicating the urgent concern of the artist himself (or, more correctly, of his message). He paints fast, he tells Bernard, for intensity (633), and in so doing he commits "mistakes . . . that a REALIST *wouldn't really make*. Certain inaccuracies of which I'm convinced myself" and which are "imperfections." Yet he knows what he is doing, and his work "will have a certain life and *raison d'être* that will overwhelm those faults — in the eyes of those who appreciate character" (528). The "certain life" here is itself a product of the "imperfections" which in the work as a whole impart something of the search for meaning, beyond decorum, convention, and technical skill. By contrast, "academic" drawings can be "Impeccable — *without faults*," but "without giving us anything new" (515), and for Vincent, as we see, academic propriety all too readily "freezes" and "petrifies" (184) the creative impulse. The "new" thing that he seeks to express by his own particular simplifications and exaggerations is, rather, a direct, compassionate, living presence offering and inviting mutual understanding, while struggling (as we all do) with limitations, imperfections, and weaknesses.

In a letter to his mother (and again echoing St. Paul), Vincent tells her that "I haven't perceived those to whom I've been most attached other than through a glass darkly" (885). That is, we do not see one another transparently, not least because "it's neither the best paintings nor the best people — in which there are no errors or bias" (465). Even God, the supreme artist, botched his creation, and this world is just "one of his studies that turned out badly" (613). Consequently, within it, we find ourselves having to go on without much self-knowledge (516), putting up with one another's faults. This opaque dimension, the unbridgeable, silent longing that we bring to even our most ardent relationships, is itself thematized in what Vincent calls real painting, the sign and presence of a humanity still in the making, unfinished, yet opening itself courageously and without pretense. "In the midst of the artistic life," he tells Theo, "there remains and it always comes back at times," a "yearning for — real life — ideal and not attainable" (611). Life, like art, is imperfect, and we know this because we can conceive of "the truly ideal." We are most ourselves, most creative, when our lives and work are courageously inspired by the ideal, while we also compassionately accept our inability to realize it.

Still, even while acknowledging the riskiness of Vincent's way of working, we should hesitate to conclude that he ignored technique simply because he favoured the unfinished and spontaneous. By contrast, he put himself through an arduous apprenticeship as a draughtsman, claiming repeatedly that drawing is the foundation of good painting. He describes how he has "been toiling solely on the figure" (347) and how much "in detail" he attended to the drawing of a leg and an arm, for "one must study a great deal and not imagine that one can do it" (353). He is scornful of the idea that art is produced by natural gifts (400) alone; instead, he admires Gustave Doré's proclaiming himself to have "the patience of an ox" — a "real artist's saying," of which Vincent approves. One can learn such patience from nature, for instance from watching the wheat grow (400), and in a memoir, his student Anton Kerssemakers describes how for weeks Vincent would focus exclusively on the drawing of hands, feet, or wooden shoes. From the start and throughout, Vincent dedicated himself patiently and with a fierce intensity of focus to what he calls the "horrors of the 'work'" (699).

But is there a contradiction between Vincent's approval of painting "in one go" (537) and his recommendations about working "for a long time and slowly" (800) in the patient acquisition of technical skill? For an answer, we might look to a notion that he came across in Eugène Delacroix, whom he revered. You must practise until you know a technique "*by heart!*" (496), says Delacroix, because then your imaginative powers will find expression in a way that transcends technique while drawing on its strengths. A violinist, a chess player, or a martial artist (for instance) understand equally well what Delacroix is getting at, and how technique, once fully assimilated, can at certain moments release a creative spontaneity which is especially powerful because it emerges from a strong foundation. Although Vincent often worked in a hurry, he reworked the same studies until he knew every shade and nuance "by heart." He describes how he would draw "repeatedly" from the model until "among the studies one will eventually come through that's something different from an ordinary study" (437) because it has some special quality of life and feeling. Technique is a necessary preparation for such "different" moments, even though they come unbidden, and when they do, one works unselfconsciously, drawing upon hard-earned skills but unaware of them. In this way, great artists "forget themselves in — being true" (551), and "one paints as if in a dream" (699), as the magic, the awakening power, the enlivening simplification, exaggeration, or telling imperfection, transfigure technique into art, so that a viewer might even be fooled into thinking that technique has played no considerable part at all.

Vincent's remarkable letters tell us a lot about the man, and are indispensable to his biographers. But they also tell us a great deal about his aims and opinions as a painter, and, in so doing, they help us to see and understand the paintings themselves. Yet the letters are not just ancillary to Vincent's graphic art; they are distinguished in their own right, demonstrating his unusual talents as a writer and thinker. In their fashion, they do what the paintings also do. They too confront and embrace us. They are direct, powerful, swirling with energy, spontaneous, often unfinished and incorrect, always infused with a dynamic, living presence that transfigures the ideas for which they argue. They are often pained and turbulent, but they are unmistakably noble, honest, and courageous. Also, in their own way they are informed by principles that Vincent had thought through again and again from different angles and by dint of tireless practice. As we see, these principles are not explored systematically or academically; rather, they are everywhere infused with Vincent's passionate and complex personality. Together, the letters and the paintings might best be thought of as synergistic — that is, the effect of their combined interaction is greater than the sum of their parts independently. Together, they are part of a single overarching project at which I have hinted here by focusing on the ideas of simplification and exaggeration, imperfection and the unfinished.

And so we return to the fact that in Vincent's case the man and his art are to an unusual degree bound up together in the hearts and minds of his admirers — as we can see any day, any season, any year in the museum in Amsterdam, where his pictures draw visitors in such abundant supply, but where the man himself, obscurely yet palpably, draws their further, respectful presence. "I . . . don't make the slightest claim to perfection" (351), Vincent admits, and "I myself will actually never think my own work finished or ready" (499). But they come nonetheless, these visitors, finding in this imperfect life and unperfected art a courage, integrity, and compassion far more humanly significant and true to life than any of the ideals which Vincent says he fails to realize.

3

The Trouble with Visions

The world's major religions have been much concerned with the idea of perfection and, especially in the main monotheistic traditions, with relationships between the one, perfect creator God and his all-too-imperfect human creatures. Rules, regulations, refinements of dogma, ritual, prayer, theology, are means of explaining how we should address the overarching mystery of the cosmos while also improving how we live our lives in relation to one another. Consequently, by faith and obedient practice, believers think that they can conduct themselves in a manner more pleasing to God than is the case with unbelievers. This is so because God's special revelation is imparted to the prophets and founders of the traditions in question (I am thinking mainly of Judaism, Christianity, Islam), and those who accept this revelation possess a saving knowledge that outsiders do not have. In turn, God's word is enshrined for posterity in the books which the monotheistic traditions hold sacred — the Hebrew and

Christian Bibles and the Qur'an. But who is to say that these books do in fact contain God's word? One principal, but not reassuring, answer is that the books themselves say so — supported by oral traditions which reaffirm that indeed what the books say is true.

I do not want to deal here with the sacred books; rather, I would like to consider the broader question of revelation itself, and of claims to special or visionary experience. As an example, I would like to deal with the remarkable book *Showings,* by the fourteenth-century Christian mystic, Julian of Norwich.

Not surprisingly, ecclesiastical authorities have often been wary of visionaries and mystics, because the special adventure in experience through which a wondrous, all-encompassing perfection is revealed to a visionary individual can have unsettling effects on the doctrines and prescriptions by which the lives of the faithful are ordered. As the mystics often tell us, the sublimity of their experiences transcends language, and it is then often touch and go as to whether this could be taken to mean that official, orthodox teachings themselves are transcended or perhaps contradicted. In short, a particular, special revelation claimed by an individual believer needs to be safely contained within the larger revelation enshrined in the sacred books — for instance, the Bible as interpreted by the church. The alternative is heresy.

And so, in investigating the truth-claims of a mystic such as Julian of Norwich, the authorities find themselves again addressing the question with which I began. How are we to know that a special revelation has occurred, or how it might enable us to live our lives in imitation of the divine perfection to which we can aspire but which we can never presume to attain?

One main problem with mystics and seers is — much as with the sacred books themselves — that you only have their word for it when they tell you they have had a vision. Writing in the seventeenth century, Benjamin Whichcote (1609–83), himself a convinced Christian with mystical inclinations, points out that in order for him to believe in the vision you say you have had, he in turn needs a vision. That is, it needs to dawn on him, as a kind of inner revelation, that you are telling the truth. Otherwise, he cannot really know.

After all, you might be mad, epileptic, migrainous, high on drugs, or have a neurological disease that has you seeing things. Perhaps St. Paul was suffering from an epileptically induced lesion in his occipital cortex when he fell off his horse on the road to Damascus and was converted. Perhaps St. John the Divine had a psychotic hallucination as a result of which he ascribed to a visiting angel the wild thing we know as the Book of Revelation.

A standard response to such suggestions is that the great influence and authority of religious texts such as Paul's letters and the Book of Revelation could not be the result of mere delusion. The coherence and staying power of these writings over the centuries are evidence that the authors were intelligently conveying a powerful message.

What, then, seems probable? First, it is unlikely that angels exist because there is no sufficient evidence for them. Second, we should assume that books are written by humans, not least because no one has observed non-human authors at work and because the case for non-human agents is made by dubious circular arguments. As Whichcote says, the claim for supernatural agency is believed because the messenger who states such a claim is believed first. Imagine a disciple telling an unbeliever, "My master speaks with angels." "How do you know?" asks the skeptic. "Fool! Would an angel lie?" That is the main case for supernatural inspiration in a nutshell — though, not surprisingly, it is often made to sound more complicated and less unreasonable.

For instance, theologians will say that they respect reason and are willing and able to engage in philosophical discussion. When they have shown themselves capable of arguing well, they then point out (correctly) that reason does not give us full enough answers. To supply the omission, they go on to claim that a special revelation has been made to some privileged human agent to whose teachings they subscribe. And so we are back where we started.

Not all theologians are equally friendly to philosophy, however, and a broad spectrum of opinion exists between anti-rationalist fundamentalists who begin by declaring the poverty of reason and liberals who all but naturalize the contents of revelation by making it appear like philosophy wearing a symbolic mask. Still, by and large, internal differences among believers have less to do with escaping the basic circular argument than with how tightly the circle is drawn. Liberal theologians cast their net widely in the attempt to include other kinds of discourse; fundamentalists make their circle small, simplifying and concentrating the main message to the virtual exclusion of other kinds of discussion. Nonetheless, in all cases the core belief in certain privileged, specially revealed facts means that there is only one centre to the circle, however large or small the circumference. By contrast, secular scientists and philosophical rationalists, who also construct their own hermeneutic circles, do not believe in privileged facts. Their claims are provisional, and they will shift their stance at the centre as the evidence requires.

All of which brings us back to delusion and the problem of whether or not mystics and seers might be psychotic, hysterical, epileptic, or afflicted by a physical disorder affecting the brain. Yet, we need to be cautious not to assume that the alternatives are just between reason and madness, sanity and illness. Imagination can also make us feel taken out of ourselves, but without causing us to be ill or impaired. As Wordsworth says, poetry is produced by our "recollection in tranquility" of heightened moments of experience, and the muse, traditionally supposed to inspire poetry, is not (as was once thought) a supernatural agent, but a psychological process.

Still, mystics who describe ecstatic visions, auditions, and other kinds of special experience do not quite fit Wordsworth's description of the creative imagination, even though there might be a good deal of overlap which we would need to assess by considering particular cases. In his remarkable historical novel *The Devils of Loudon,* Aldous Huxley gives a harrowing account of religious hysteria, and it is

34

clear that Huxley's own imaginative powers are quite different from the deranged imaginations of the hysterical nuns he describes. Yet Huxley would also be the first to agree that not all mystics are like these nuns. St. Teresa of Ávila describes extraordinary visions and ecstatic raptures, but as a writer and administrator she was hard-headed, practical, and highly intelligent. She is not quite a poet like Wordsworth, but it is not easy to conclude, either, that she was merely another of Huxley's hysterics.

In his much-admired book, *The Man Who Mistook His Wife for a Hat* (New York: Harper & Row, Perennial Library ed., 1987), Oliver Sacks describes a wide range of perceptual states hovering uncertainly between neurological disorder, creative imagination, and spirituality. We learn about a man who loses his ability to recognize objects visually but deploys his remarkable musical skills to keep his life in order. A woman suffers a thrombosis in her right temporal lobe and experiences a sudden "musical epilepsy" (131), as a result of which her head becomes filled with Irish songs. As it turns out, her hallucinations had a healing effect. The woman had been orphaned in Ireland at a young age and sent to America. She had lost all memory of her early childhood, an omission that pained her. But the music brought back precise recollections that enabled her to make sense of her early, lost years, and Sacks sees the woman's seizures as "a kind of 'conversion,' giving a centre to a centreless life" (145).

Sacks' main examples are drawn from his clinical practice, but he devotes some pages also to the twelfth-century mystic Hildegard of Bingen (1098–1179), who has provided written descriptions and pictorial illustrations of her visions. Sacks states that Hildegard was "indisputably migrainous" (168). That is, migraine headaches caused her visions, and "she experienced a shower of phosphenes in transit across the visual field, their passage being succeeded by a negative scotoma" (169). Yet Sacks qualifies his own diagnosis, going on to point out that Hildegard's visions "were instrumental in directing her towards a life of holiness and mysticism" (169). In her case, the physical illness became "the substrate of a supreme ecstatic inspiration," and Sacks looks to the great Russian novelist, Fyodor Dostoevsky, for a similar example.

It seems, then, that clear lines cannot be drawn in all cases between physiological or neurological disorders, the creative imagination, and visionary experience of a religious kind. Complex interlacements might occur, differently configured in a wide variety of cases, each of which requires individual assessment. Among theologians, especially in pre-modern times, this kind of assessment was known as "discernment of spirits," a precursor, as it were, of modern psychoanalysis. Certainly, mystics and their spiritual advisors knew very well that imagination can deceive and that illness can cause delusions; consequently, not all claims to mystical experience were taken at face value. John of the Cross (1542-91) and Teresa of Ávila (1515-82) both warn against false visions, which Madame Guyon (1648-1717) also describes as dangerously seductive: "These [ecstasies] arise from a sensible relish, and may be termed a kind of spiritual sensuality, wherein the soul letting itself go too far by reason of the sweetness it finds, falls imperceptibly into decay" (*The Devout Christian*, "Ecstasies").

One main indicator for spiritual advisors of the difference between a genuinely ecstatic experience and the "spiritual sensuality" described by Madame Guyon is whether or not a person is morally improved, mentally stable, humble, charitable, and competent in day-to-day life. If a visionary experience produces such results, which can be witnessed and assessed by others, then the person might be judged trustworthy, and a Benjamin Whichcote moment can occur: we will "see" that the experience is authentic. Even if there is an organic or neurological determinant at work, this does not diminish the integrity of the moral or psychological consequences, as Sacks is keen to point out (130). Hildegard could not be expected to know about the shower of phosphenes causing her migrainous visions, but we can go on affirming the beauty and insight of her writing as well as her moral integrity without supposing that these qualities are diminished because she had migraines, or that a special, supernatural intervention had occurred.

Are the mystics then wrong about God? Perhaps they are, though it depends on what is meant by God. One common assertion among mystical writers is that their experience of the divine mystery is beyond words or description. Angela of Foligno (c. 1248–1309) says that although "the soul delighteth unspeakably" in its experience of the divine presence, "yet it beholdeth naught which can be related by the tongue or imagined in the heart" (*The Divine Consolation*, Treatise III, Seventh Vision), and Nicholas of Cusa (1401–64) tells us, "This alone I know, that I know not what I see, and never can know. And I know not how to name thee because I know not what Thou art" (*The Vision of God*, chap. 13). Statements such as these are not uncommon in the literature, but a thoughtful atheist would find no difficulty in also affirming opinions like these, for of course the universe is mysterious and awe-inspiring and our presence in it is unspeakably wonderful and strange. Not surprisingly, mystics often make ecclesiastical authorities uneasy by seeming to override the patiently worked-out creeds and prescriptions to which true believers subscribe. In Christian tradition, spiritual writers have needed to be careful to provide reassurances of their orthodoxy in order to avoid being considered heretical and perhaps being introduced to the truth-serum of physical pain. As I have said, discernment in these matters requires attention to individual cases, so let us briefly consider Julian of Norwich (1342–after 1416), whose book *Showings* (sometimes called *Revelations*) offers a remarkable account of a visionary experience.

We know very little about the author of *Showings*. She was attached to the church of St. Julian, in Norwich, a town in northern England where she lived an enclosed life as an anchoress, taking her name from her place of habitation — both the church and the town; thus, Julian of Norwich. She has left two accounts (usually referred to as the short and long texts) of an intense vision she experienced while she lay seriously ill in May 1373. Some readers are inclined to think that the long text expands on the short version in which Julian first recorded her experiences, but there is no evidence for this. The main point is that Julian's book survives as a spiritual classic, continuing to have a devoted readership.

Julian tells us that she was thirty and a half years old when she became ill in May 1373. She was at the point of death, she says, and lay gazing at a crucifix. Then everything went dark, except for the crucifix, which remained strangely illuminated, and Julian experienced Christ's agony in an acutely painful way. At the point of extremity when she felt she could bear no more, a great transformation occurred and she was enveloped in divine love and blessedness, with the assurance of the now-famous words (incorporated by T.S. Eliot into his wonderful late poem, *The Four Quartets*): "All shall be well." Julian's visions lasted for more than thirty hours, and in her book she describes them and considers their implications.

Even a brief glance at the text of *Showings* reveals Julian's concern not to offend against the teachings of "Holy Church." She keeps insisting that "in everything I believe as Holy Church preaches and teaches" (chap. 9, 192), and she repeats this assurance so insistently that it is hard not to feel an anxiety that her visions are, at certain points, not exactly what "Holy Church" would want to hear.

A number of key emphases make Julian's experiences so distinctly her own as to be, indeed, on the edge of orthodoxy. First, she claims that there is no anger in God, who does not blame us and does not forgive us, and although she wanted to learn more about hell and purgatory, she saw nothing to indicate that they exist. Second, she comes close to affirming universal salvation — the idea that eventually everyone will be saved; only then can "every kind of thing . . . be well" (chap. 32, 233), as the Lord promised. Third, she insists on God's maternal nature, and although other Christian writers had dealt with this idea, Julian's treatment of it is unusual. She suggests that Jesus is our mother because he takes on our sensuality in order to raise us up to God (chap. 59, 295), and she offers daring descriptions of how "our true Mother Jesus" at first carries us within himself, then feeds us with himself and lays us on his breast "through his sweet open side" (chap. 60, 298).

Julian's book is frequently startling, arresting, and inventive, but it is also clear-headed and astute. For instance, she acknowledges the church teaching that "many creatures will be damned" (chap. 32, 233) and "eternally condemned to hell" (chap. 32, 233), and she does not fudge the fact that a contradiction exists between this teaching and her own visions. If there is hell, she points out, "it seemed to me that it was impossible that every kind of thing should be well, as our Lord revealed at this time" (chap. 32, 233). Reflecting further, Julian decides that she must "stand firm" behind her vision, even while also submitting to the church. The Lord then gives her a reassurance which confirms the contradiction, allowing it to stand unresolved: "What is impossible to you is not impossible to me." Two versions of the circular argument are interestingly at work here. First, Julian has claimed that her vision is true because the Lord spoke to her (and would the Lord lie?). Second, the Lord addresses the contradiction between her visions and the teachings of Holy Church by telling her that he will resolve the matter in due course. Meanwhile, it is quite all right for her to go on living with the contradiction (and, again, would the Lord lie, even if what he says doesn't make a lot of sense?).

Elsewhere, Julian states on two occasions that the Lord assured her that she was not having hallucinations (chap. 68, 314); (chap. 70, 317). But again, how are we to know that such a claim is true? As we might expect, the answer is that the book tells us so. And then, what about Julian's illness, which, she says, brought her close to death? What might Oliver Sacks be able to tell us, had he been there? It seems likely that Julian's visions were caused by her illness in much the same way as Hildegard's migraines produced the shower of phosphenes in her visual field. Even so, as Sacks goes on to say about Hildegard, Dostoevsky, and the woman who heard Irish songs, the illness does not vitiate the "psychological or spiritual significance" of the experiences in question.

In summary, it is probable that Julian's illness caused her visions, but, in turn, these remained profoundly significant. Understandably, she set out to describe and interpret her special experience in the only language available, namely, that provided by Holy Church. In so doing, she affirmed a universal compassion that makes all things well and is incompatible with hell and damnation. She needed to be courageous to make known this part of her message, and she ran a risk in doing so. The reality that transcends and subsumes creeds, theologies, and religious orthodoxies remains, as always, mysteriously beyond description, but Julian's message of compassion, as well as her defiance, contain a moral energy for which we can go on admiring her without having to resolve the gap between our intuitions of the cosmic mystery and our actual, painfully imperfect understandings. Ralph Waldo Emerson says that God offers to each of us a choice between truth and repose, and we can take whichever we please but we cannot have both. Among other things, Emerson might be reminding us that one problem with circular arguments such as those that support claims to a special revelation is that their perfection of form provides a too-easy repose, and, consequently, a temptation to self-righteousness about which religious believers especially need to remain concerned. Julian would understand.

_____

4

Northern Ireland, Sri Lanka, and Regressive Inversion

Love your enemies, do good to those
who hate you, bless those who curse
you, pray for those who abuse you.
    Luke 6:27-30

Hatreds do not ever cease in this
world by hating, but by love; this
is an eternal truth.
    Dhammapada 1:5

There is no reason why people who love their neighbour for religious reasons should not also work to promote the common good by
political means. The politics can remain secular even though a commitment to justice and compassion might (for some people) continue
to have roots in religious conviction. The fact that these roots are, as

it were, beneath the surface does not mean that they lack the kind of energy that can be deployed to further a political cause. For instance, in confronting tyranny and oppression, a religious conviction might be inspiring and liberating; but also it might not, and religion can turn out to be as tyrannical as the political oppressions which, in some circumstances, it opposes. As history shows, there is no end to the catalogue of horrors perpetrated in God's name.

There are no simple answers here, and much depends on particular circumstances and on the status of a believer's understanding. Yet it is a good thing that a secular critique remains sufficiently robust to insist that the common good can be as well served by non-religious people as by religious ones. In themselves, religious claims are not proven true by, for instance, a believer's resistance to injustice. Morality remains the main criterion against which the practical value of a religious belief can be assessed, rather than the reverse — which is to say, religious beliefs about supernatural agency are not the arbiters of morality.

Still, these distinctions are easily confused or confusing, and the interplay between religion and politics is volatile, liable to go badly in a wide variety of ways. In the following pages I want to focus on one of these ways, which, for convenience, I will call "regressive inversion," and which develops directly from the universalizing idealism of religion itself.

In brief, regressive inversion occurs when a universalizing religious vision is redeployed to support special interests despite the contradiction entailed in doing so. In the political arena, the consequences of regressive inversion are frequently disastrous, and my examples are from the recent histories of Northern Ireland and Sri Lanka, two islands on different sides of the world, in both of which religion (Christianity and Buddhism, respectively) has been enmeshed in politics in the unfortunate manner I have just described. One result is that the ethnic dimensions of both conflicts are intensified — the very thing that the teachings of Jesus and the Buddha especially sought to prevent. Both preached a universal morality, not dependent on ties to kin, caste, or tribe, but based on the inner disposition of each individual person. And so the gospels tell how Jesus, Prince of Peace, taught compassion, forgiveness, and love of our neighbour. Some five hundred years earlier, another Prince — Siddhartha Gautama — found enlightenment as a Buddha and likewise declared a message of compassion and non-violence. In this shared enterprise, Jesus and the Buddha indeed are brothers — but in a spiritual sense, in contrast to the biological variety, on which, as it happens, neither Jesus nor the Buddha was especially keen.

In Matthew's gospel, as Jesus fulminates against the "generation of vipers" around him, his mother and brethren arrive and Jesus is informed. But he is neither courteous nor gracious; instead he asks, combatively, "Who is my mother? And who are my brethren?" To answer his own question he points to his disciples: "Behold my mother and my brethren. For whosoever shall do the will of my Father which is in heaven, the same is my brother, and sister, and mother" (Matt. 12:48-50).

Jesus's new family was soon to develop into a hybrid collection, comprising people from all nations, including many individuals written off in the eyes of the world as outsiders, pariahs, and rejects. Whoever got the core message, regardless of social status, family ties, or nationality, could belong in this revolutionary family of love.

In an event known as the Great Renunciation, Prince Siddhartha likewise sought a new understanding of human solidarity. In so doing, he abandoned his wife and child, turning his back on family, parents, and princely duties as he set out alone on a spiritual search. Eventually, as an enlightened Buddha, he formed his own band of brothers (and, eventually, sisters) — the *bhikkhus,* or monks, brought together as a spiritual family regardless of caste, social status, or tribal affiliation.

Still, neither the Buddha nor Jesus condemned family life outright. After all, the family provides our basic material needs — what the early Marx describes as our "species being," consisting of such things as food, shelter, security, and a healthy environment. But although they do not ignore our need for basic nurture, the Buddha and Jesus want to instill a kind of understanding that would enable us to transcend our primary loyalties to the family and kin group. We are to do this by embracing a universal morality that requires the assent of autonomous individuals, unrestricted by an affiliation with kin, caste, tribe, or nation. Consequently, despite disagreements on other matters, Buddhists and Christians enjoin a similar universal, unconditional compassion, non-violence, and selflessness.

What happens, then, in places such as Northern Ireland (where the majority describe themselves as Christian), and Sri Lanka (where the majority describe themselves as Buddhist), when religion becomes a badge of ethnically based partisanship in violent civil conflicts that have cost thousands of lives?

First, when the identity of an ethnic group is marked by the nominal allegiance of its members to religion, it is easy to see how the group itself can appear sacrosanct to its members. This is not surprising — tribal gods, after all, have paraded and war-danced their way through history. But when the core values of religions such as Christianity and Buddhism are annexed to ethnicity, a second, highly dangerous complexity arises.

As we see, the Buddha and Jesus invite us to an ideal universal vision entailing boundless aspirations and unconditional commitments. When such all-encompassing energies are deployed to supercharge the basic passions associated with group loyalty — the very passions that the universal religious ideal was expressly designed to transcend — they become especially dangerous. In short, an inversion of value occurs when highly idealized spiritual aspirations are made the servant of regressive impulses to anger and revenge. The process by which this occurs is what I mean by "regressive inversion." It is *regressive* insofar as it reaffirms an exclusive group identity, and it entails an *inversion* of value insofar as it derives power from the languages of transcendence, informed as these are by aspirations to an absolute liberation and an ideal perfection.

There is a long tradition in Irish Republicanism of annexing religious absolutes to the tribal cause in this way, as became increasingly evident during the civil unrest — the Northern Ireland Troubles — which lasted, roughly, from the late 1960s until the Good Friday Agreement of 1998. For instance, prison literature and iconography at the time of the Hunger Strikes of 1980 and 1981 (published interviews, smuggled documents, partisan commentary, memoirs, mural paintings) show an infusion of Republican ideals with the language and imagery of religious sacrifice and redemption, an extravagant mixture of Celtic sentimentality and Counter-Reformation Catholicism. The armed struggle, rosary beads, the tricolour, resurrection (of an oppressed people), the suffering savior, and Republican heroism interpenetrate in a blood-stirring (or blood-curdling, depending on your point of view) farrago, drenched with emotionalism and dangerous confusions. One result is that the religious iconography is less a protest against political injustice than an assertion of Ireland's "real" culture, the possession especially of its Catholic and Celtic people, and, despite its official socialist declarations, Republicanism has lapsed too frequently into crude sectarianism.

In the opposite camp, the Ulster Loyalist equivalent is resolutely Protestant, more directly propositional, and uncompromisingly direct. Yet Loyalism displays its own brand of sentimental heroism, often fancifully based on the idea of a chosen Israel beleaguered by foes but undaunted, steadfast, and true. In her appropriately titled *Watchmen in Sion* (Derry: Field Day Theatre Company, 1985), Marianne Elliott cites a handbill produced in 1971, declaring how "the enemies of our faith and freedom are determined to destroy the state of Northern Ireland and thereby enslave the people of God." Here, a supposedly modern, secular, democratic state is sacralized, and by defending Northern Ireland, God's (Protestant) people are to prevent the equivalent of another Babylonian captivity. As with the Hunger Strikes, this example shows how readily the core concepts of a world-transcending religious idealism are hijacked and redeployed in the service of a merely exclusivist chauvinism. Even the usually patient Jesus might be forgiven a moment of (regressive) exasperation.

Like Ireland, Sri Lanka is an island riven by violence, and again religion plays a key part in the definition of ethnic identity. Especially since independence from Britain in 1948, the majority Sinhalese Buddhists have stood opposed to a Tamil minority who want a separate state or some other devolved arrangement acknowledging their autonomy. The Tamil agenda is mainly secessionist, but most Tamils are Hindu, a fact which helps to clarify for the Sinhalese their own distinct identity as Buddhists. On both sides, violence has been appalling, but I am interested here mainly in Buddhism, and in how regressive inversion affects Sinhalese Buddhist nationalism in a way that parallels what we find in Northern Ireland.

A twentieth-century revival of interest in the claims of an ancient Sri Lankan Buddhist chronicle, the *Mahavamsa* (c. 6th century CE) has especially helped to shape a Sinhalese nationalism dedicated to making Buddhism the state religion and Sinhalese the official language. Protests were registered, mainly by Tamils, but the situation deteriorated and thirty years of violence ensued. By and large, Sinhalese hegemony has prevailed, though instead of becoming the state religion, Buddhism was granted the status of "foremost religion," and Tamil has been designated a "national language," in contrast to Sinhala, which is "official" as well as "national."

Briefly, the *Mahavamsa* tells how Buddhism came to Sri Lanka in the third century CE. Throughout, the chronicle insists that religion and territory are fused in the historical destiny of the Sinhalese people. We also learn about a decisive battle between the ancient Buddhist hero Dutthagamini and his Tamil opponent, Elara. Supported by the *Sangha* (the community of Buddhist monks), Dutthagamini prevailed, carrying a relic of the Buddha on his spear. Later, he worried about the loss of life he had caused, but the monks assured him that those he had killed were almost entirely non-Buddhist, and so his conscience should not be uneasy. What the monks say has (understandably) exerted a considerable fascination upon commentators:

46

From this deed rises no hindrance in thy way to heaven. Only one and a half human beings have been slain here by thee, O lord of men. The one had come unto the (three) refuges, the other had taken on himself the five precepts. Unbelievers and men of evil life were the rest, not more to be esteemed than beasts. But as for thee, thou wilt bring glory to the doctrine of the Buddha in manifold ways; therefore, cast away care from the heart, O ruler of men! (178)

That is, Dutthagamini can rest easy because there was only one committed Buddhist and one half-hearted Buddhist among the enemy troops; the rest were to be considered not human at all, "not more to be esteemed than beasts." The main point is the honour Dutthagamini brings "to the doctrine of the Buddha," and this greater good justifies the violence required to bring it about.

The conviction recorded in the *Mahavamsa* that the Sinhalese people are special custodians of Buddhism and that the nation and the religion thrive together and should be defended together, by armed force if necessary, was widely invoked in the Sinhalese Buddhist revival that occurred around the time of independence in 1948. Walpola Rahula's *The Heritage of the Bhikkhu* (New York: Grove Press, 1974; first published 1946) is a seminal document in this movement. Rahula, himself a *bhikkhu,* commends the *Mahavamsa* and praises Dutthagamini for "liberating the nation from a foreign yoke" (20). He goes on to argue that "the nation and the religion have to move together" (95), and his passionate, learned argument plays everywhere on the emotional appeal of such things as ancient lineage, blood-identity, and rightful inheritance. Throughout, ethnic nationalism once more deploys a universalizing vision in a way that dangerously inverts the very priorities the Buddha had preached long and hard to establish.

The Lord Buddha and the Lord Jesus are therefore appropriated alike to an exclusionist cause, leaders now of a warlike company of brothers inspired by a heady sense of tribal solidarity. In a situation where an ethnic minority might find itself identified by religion and then subjected to persecution, such a sense of common identity can be a means of resisting injustice. But it is all too seductive a temptation to turn this kind of solidarity into an assertion of the God-ordained special interests of the group, exclusive of outsiders. By such means, wars of resistance can turn into tyrannies, and regressive inversion helps to explain how such a thing can occur, as the vision of an ideal perfection is redeployed in the service of an all-too-imperfect exclusionism which the ideal itself denounces.

In such matters, the cross-currents are complex and shifting, and require careful navigation. Here I have drawn attention to one current which is especially dangerous. In the next chapter I would like to consider another, different example of how religious perfectionism can create a wilderness around itself, making an already imperfect world a great deal more troubled and imperfect still.

5

Osama, Theo, and the
Burnt Fool's Bandaged Finger

In the previous chapter I suggested that the universal ideals of religions such as Christianity and Buddhism can be deployed to reinforce a merely exclusive chauvinism. Here I want to consider an extension of this idea, focusing on how a conviction of perfect righteousness can also be a perfect incentive to murder.

I would like to consider two examples. The first deals with a letter from Osama bin Laden to the American people in 2002. The second focuses on a letter pinned to the murdered body of Theo Van Gogh in Amsterdam in 2004. Both are examples of Islamist jihadism in action, and both are extreme cases which do not represent the opinions and attitudes of most Muslims any more than the depredations of Northern Irish and Sri Lankan paramilitaries represent the attitudes and opinions of most Christians and Buddhists. Still, the fact remains that the one perfect God who imparts righteousness to the faithful runs the risk of having some all-too-true believers turn into monsters. If this is a risk that God wants to take, it deserves scrutiny, not least by the community of believers themselves.

A few days before the US presidential election of 2004, Osama bin Laden released a videotaped message to the Al Jazeera network, from where it made its way to the main US news media. Supposedly addressing the "American people," the message posed some difficulties for the US journalists who received it. On the one hand, they did not want to suppress it; on the other, they did not want it to have an impact on the election.

And so, by and large, the major networks settled for presenting a video clip of an unusually spectral-looking bin Laden, together with an audio translation of the least provocative few lines of his message: "I tell you in truth, that your security is not in the hands of Kerry, nor Bush, nor al-Qaida. No. Your security is in your own hands. And every state that doesn't play with our security has automatically guaranteed its own security." For their part, Kerry and Bush responded with eager dismissals of anything the bogeyman might have to say, and the political campaigns rolled on, apparently unimpeded, to the grisly conclusion of 2 November.

The full transcript of bin Laden's speech allows us to realize that he had a good deal more to say than the sound bites offered by the main broadcast media at the time when the speech was delivered. In four single-spaced pages, he makes substantive points about US foreign policy and provides some reflections on 9/11.

Briefly, we learn that the attack on the United States occurred because of "the oppression and tyranny of the American/Israel coalition," and, in particular, because of the 1982 Israeli invasion of Lebanon, supported by the US Sixth Fleet. During the bombardment, many civilians were killed, including high-rise apartment dwellers, and bin Laden smugly notices a pleasing symmetry when high-rise buildings were also destroyed in Manhattan in 2001.

A list of further accusations goes on to condemn the United States for supporting corrupt regimes, pillaging oil, and being responsible for the deaths of "millions" of children as a result of the embargo on Iraq. Then, in an almost witty moment bin Laden pauses to repudiate Bush's claim that the 9/11 attacks occurred "because we hate freedom." If this is so, Bush should "explain to us why we don't strike for example — Sweden?" Presumably, the true freedom-loving nations of northern Europe (to Sweden we could add the likes of Norway, Denmark and, well, yes, Holland) are exempt because they practice what they preach — unlike the bullying, hypocritical Americans.

So far, these points are political, yet the message as a whole gives us more than bin Laden-the-reasonable pursuing a political cause. A further, chillingly unsettling dimension declares itself first in a certain casualness or remoteness, born of bin Laden's unhesitating assurance that a God-ordained, grand plan is being realized and all else besides is incidental. A lethally unperturbed assurance seeps everywhere through the pores of his rhetoric, as when he notices the pleasing symmetry between the falling towers of Lebanon and Manhattan or when he confides that he perceives a contrite self-reproof in "the gestures" of those killed as the Manhattan towers fell, at which time he heard the dying confess: "How mistaken we were to have allowed the White House to implement its aggressive foreign policy against the weak without supervision." That is, the victims of 9/11 are on bin Laden's side after all, acknowledging their mistakes, at last brought to their senses — saved in the end by being destroyed by him. To round out this solemnly pornographic fantasy, bin Laden ends with an all-too-familiar claim: "Allah is our Guardian and Helper, while you have no Guardian and Helper." Which is to say, God is with al Qaeda but has abandoned the United States. Throughout, of course, the Almighty is copiously thanked for having chosen so well.

Faced with this disturbing mix, we might ask whether bin Laden invokes religion mainly to infuse and energize a political message or whether his political grievances are a stalking horse for aspirations to a theocracy within which unbelievers are by definition the enemy.

I want to think that the first of these alternatives is the case, even though to assume this might be yet another secular liberal delusion. Besides, the alternatives are not mutually exclusive, and people frequently oscillate, unwilling to surrender one of these poles entirely in favour of the other. Thus, at one moment a person might give priority to the sublime directives of the Almighty and, at another, feel more strongly the immediate urgencies of politics.

For his part, bin Laden doubtless understands the advantage of keeping his liberal secular readers guessing about such issues, if only to make it easier to wrong-foot them. Yet, even the most flummoxed, wrong-footed liberal has much less to guess about when it comes to the murder of Theo Van Gogh, ritually slaughtered in the name of Islam on an Amsterdam street on 2 November 2004, and left with a five-page letter stabbed into his body. Holland, "the beating liberal heart of Europe," as a commentator says, has hardly found itself immune to those who think it a good idea to kill unbelievers, especially if their opinions give offence.

Theo Van Gogh (great-grandnephew of the painter, Vincent) was an *avant-garde* artist, TV personality, and provocateur-at-large — a carnivalesque "ram of fat" (as he called himself) who routinely presented his TV guests with a cactus plant to remind them of their prickly encounters with him. He trained his fetid breath first on Christians, and then Jews, before targeting Muslims — especially through a short (eleven-minute) film about the mistreatment of Islamic women. The film, entitled *Submission,* was scripted by the Dutch-Somali, ex-Muslim, female member of parliament, Ayaan Hirsi Ali. It caused a stir, and Van Gogh received threats, which he shrugged off, convinced that nobody would harm "the village idiot." In short, he understood his function as a carnivalesque figure, and once told an interviewer, "I'm a piece of shit — but so are you." His main message lies, roughly, there, and in the garrulous, insulting rough-and-tumble of his prickly brand of satire, he assumed that the freedom to offend and otherwise expose the ludicrous aspects of institutional religion is one mainstay of a secular freedom of expression. By and large, the

Dutch retain close enough memories of the Nazi occupation to be willing to put up with a lot in the name of this kind of freedom, and Theo Van Gogh, relative of a Dutch icon, freewheeling on his Dutch bike along Linnaeusstraat in the centre of liberal Amsterdam, was the symbol and embodiment of that spirit of toleration.

Van Gogh's killer, Mohammed Bouyeri, was a twenty-six-year-old Dutch-Moroccan. He shot Theo several times and then sawed through his neck with a butcher knife, attempting to decapitate him. Finally, he stuck the knife into the dead man's chest and used another knife to stab a letter into the body. Bouyeri apparently thought that a subsequent shootout with police would send him off to his reward in paradise (he carried a note in his pocket to that effect and he later confirmed the point in court), but the police uncooperatively shot him in the legs and took him in.

As it turns out, Bouyeri did not operate alone, but as a member of a group, labelled by the police the "Hofstad Network." Briefly, as Bouyeri became increasingly drawn to militant extremism he found a small number of like-minded friends. Also, as Ian Buruma shows in *Murder in Amsterdam* (New York: Penguin, 2006), he fell under the influence of a radical Syrian Muslim preacher, Mohammad Radwan Alissa (a.k.a. Abou Khaled). Among other things, the Syrian cleric maintained that anyone who did not live by the divine law (sharia) as a true believer, should be killed (210). Bouyeri took this message to heart, and posted his views on the internet, for instance announcing that sharia will replace every "false human system" (meaning especially liberal democracy) and will "wipe this type of system from the face of the earth" (212). The internet opened up Bouyeri's small group to an international pool of like-minded violent jihadists, and the Hofstad Network may have had further links to other European organizations, shaped, in turn, by the divinely inspired activities of al Qaeda.

The five-page letter knifed into Theo's body begins (as does bin Laden's message) by assuring us that "there is no aggression except against the aggressors." In this case, the principal aggressor is Ayaan

Hirsi Ali, to whom the letter is addressed, threatening her life. In scripting Van Gogh's film, in giving up her religion, in her efforts as a politician to change Dutch immigration law, and in doing all this as a woman, she is, in Bouyeri's view, a "soldier of evil" on a "crusade" against Islam. But the net soon gets thrown wider, as Bouyeri complains that "Dutch politics is dominated by many Jews," and he points to the mayor of Amsterdam (Job Cohen) as an example. In turn, this anti-Semitic meander prefaces a further denunciation of, basically, anyone at all opposed to Islam, building up to the following mantic bit of trumpery:

> I know for sure that you, Oh America will go under;
> I know for sure that you, Oh Europe will go under;
> I know for sure that you, Oh Holland will go under;
> I know for sure that you, Oh Hirsi Ali will go under;
> I know for sure that you, Oh unbelieving fundamentalist will go under.

There's an escalation for you, and it's worth noting that not just Europe and America are marked for the same fate as Theo, but any unbeliever at all. In case there might be some lingering doubt, we are assured also that there will be "No discussion, no demonstrations, no parades, no petitions; merely DEATH shall separate Truth from the Lie." One report has it that the wounded Van Gogh made a final appeal to his assailant, saying, "Don't do it. We can still talk about it." But this last redoubt of reason seeking an accommodation fell on deaf ears; it was, after all, addressed to someone who had already made clear in writing that he couldn't be talked to.

And so things are simplified, and one result is that in the Netherlands an alliance rapidly began taking shape between church-going Calvinist conservatives and liberal supporters of the country's tolerant laws about drugs, prostitution, and gay marriage. Extremes meet, as even the strongest internal differences yield to a perceived need to maintain the way of life that made the internal differences possible in the first place.

Should another event resembling 9/11 occur in the United States, a rapid alliance would also likely form, as in the Netherlands, between religious conservatives and the liberal secularists who usually oppose them. There would then be even less guesswork than at present about whether or not bin Laden has a political point to make, and the evangelicals who constituted George Bush's political base would feel themselves more than ever vindicated. As Bruce Bartlett (advisor to Ronald Reagan and the first President Bush) told *New York Times* reporter Ron Suskind: "This is why George W. Bush is so clear-eyed about al Qaeda and the Islamic fundamentalist enemy. He believes you have to kill them all. They can't be persuaded, that they are extremists, driven by a dark vision. He understands them because he is just like them."

One of the best books on the recent Northern Ireland conflict is Richard Davis's *Mirror Hate* (Aldershot: Dartmouth, 1994), and, among other things, it can help to clarify some implications of Bartlett's remark. In this elegant and telling analysis Davis shows that although Republican and Loyalist paramilitaries are enemies, they also mirror one another. The enmity in itself is not difficult to describe because it is plainly declared by the opposed factions and their propagandists. But a further process of "unconscious convergence," whereby the opposed factions come to resemble one another, is more difficult to discern. That is, if we hate with sufficient intensity, we unwittingly become like our enemy, mirroring our enemy's strategies and our enemy's thinking. And in this "symbiotic antagonism," says Davis, the simplifications of propaganda readily triumph over "humanity and common sense."

In Northern Ireland, the Good Friday Agreement of 1998 represents, among other things, a heroic effort to transcend the "symbiotic antagonism" Davis describes, and to open up a secular space for many-sided discussions in search of reasonable political accommodations. *Murder in Amsterdam,* Buruma's excellent study on the death of Theo Van Gogh, seeks to open up the same kind of space for discussions about the Netherlands, where, as he says, "there was something unhinged" (10) in the winter of 2004, in the wake of the murder. And as the internationalizing of an extreme form of violent religious universalism gains momentum, small countries like Ireland and the Netherlands might be weather vanes, worth the world's careful attention — even though, history being as it is, the likes of Osama and Dubya and the true believers clustering in their wake will have their minds set on their own exclusive versions of who the real enemy is.

As Kipling has it, as always "the burnt Fool's bandaged finger goes wabbling back to the fire," as the self-righteous undertake to justify themselves yet again by invoking a perfect creator while getting on with destroying the creatures who, we are told, are made in his image. This is not to deny that bin Laden has political points to make, or that Bush should not have been outraged by the events of 9/11. Some argue that if there were no political injustice on the part of the West there would be no Islamist violence, but it is impossible to judge how much truth there might be in such an assertion. This is so because we are never short either of political injustice or of religious megalomaniacs convinced of their perfect right to lay waste around them in God's name in the attempt to set it right.

6

What the Buddha Didn't Say

The world's major religions derive a good deal of authority from their success in promoting the message that ordinary people are unenlightened and in need of special instruction. In turn, this special instruction offers the prospect of a perfect happiness or liberation, requiring certain beliefs and practices on the part of the faithful. The major religions have also developed ways to mediate between the ideal perfection they enjoin and the far-from-ideal imperfections of the actual world in which they operate. Frequently, this mediation draws on imagination rather than direct, dogmatic instruction, as we see, for instance, in ecclesiastical ornament, architecture, and music. But language also is often used imaginatively to impart religious knowledge to people for whom direct instruction would be insufficiently effective. The literary dimension of the great religious books themselves can show how this kind of imaginative discourse operates, as story, parable, and dialogue are deployed to bring people to see in fresh ways, and thereby perhaps also to discover their own unacknowledged prejudices and preconceptions. In short, imaginative discourse is a way of not saying a thing directly in order to engage more effectively with people's imperfect understandings.

In this light, I want to consider some aspects of Buddhism. The Buddha's core teachings (as they are stated, for instance, in the Pali Canon) are austere, clear, and unflinchingly direct. They are supplemented by numerous plainly stated rules and classifications designed to clarify the Buddha's main teachings and to enable his disciples to live accordingly. But the Buddha also teaches through dialogue, engaging with people who oppose, resist, or misunderstand what he has to say, and in such situations he teaches by not saying directly what he means. In so doing, he uses imagination to bridge the gap between the perfection to which we aspire and the imperfections that impede our enlightenment. But first, let me say a little about the main Buddhist teachings and the vision they present of a perfect liberation from the sufferings and injustices of the world.

Buddhism comes in many varieties, but they all offer the same advice: attachment, we are to know, causes suffering. When we get attached to things through desire or craving (*tanha*), or when we cling to the objects of desire (or to desire itself), the result is *dukkha*. This word is usually translated as "suffering," but has connotations also of "dissatisfaction" and "impermanence."

The Buddha tells us that *dukkha* ceases only when we extinguish *tanha*. That is, when the fires of craving are blown out, our attachments no longer bind us and we attain enlightenment and liberation (*nirvana*). Let it all go, says the Buddha, and test the results for yourself (or whatever happens to yourself when you let that go too). "Thus," he says, "I have taught you the unconditioned and the path leading to the unconditioned. . . . This is our instruction to you" (CD, II).

Yet the simplicity here is deceptive. Non-attachment might easily be mistaken for indifference, which would preclude the key Buddhist virtue of compassion. Also, the wholly unconditioned (*nirvana*) should not be imagined as if, somehow, "we" experience it: after all, if it is unconditioned it is beyond experience. Learning how to be non-attached therefore requires the practice of virtue (compassionate action), and finding a way to the unconditioned requires meditation (bringing us beyond the illusions of self). And so the path to liberation and enlightenment lies through an interplay between moral engagement and contemplative detachment. Negotiating this interplay calls, in turn, for a high degree of skill and discernment, not least because experience does not simply conform to the ideas or principles by which we would regulate it. Consider the following.

In his remarkable autobiographical reflection, *Going Buddhist* (London: Short Books, 2004), Peter Conradi relates a story he heard in Poland about the deportation of Jews to the gas chambers at Treblinka. The families who had been rounded up in the city square knew that they would not return from the place to which the cattle trucks would take them:

> In the square the terrified, ill-nourished women from the ghetto passed their babies over their heads from one to another set of upraised hands — as I saw it in my mind's eye, with care, though presumably also with haste — towards a high wall enclosing them. They were thrown over to the other side, where pious Catholic Polish women waited and caught, collected and brought them up as gentiles. (179)

The core of this horrifying little narrative is the plight of the mothers passing their babies, not just over the wall, but to the other pairs of hands conveying them there. As Conradi says, thinking about it "stops my mind" (180). But in what sense might a Buddhist describe the mother's action as an example of "non-attachment"? Could we imagine the mothers saying, yes, attachment brings pain and it is better for us not to feel our loss? Clearly not. The mothers' loss is lacerating, and the literal non-attachment between mother and child causes barely imaginable anguish.

Yet the story does not just horrify, because courage and compassion manage also to register their own kind of protest. Just as the agents of destruction depersonalize their victims, herding them like cattle, so, by contrast, the mothers and their helpers become for a brief time, as it were, transpersonal, reaching beyond self-preservation, beyond their individual concerns, in order to rescue the babies. Sorrow indeed persists, tragic grief and loss prevail — almost, but not quite.

In another, very different narrative about letting go, *Flight to Arras* (New York, 1942), Antoine de Saint-Exupéry describes a dangerous mission that he flew as an aviator during World War II. When his plane was struck by anti-aircraft fire, he felt he would not survive. The enemy shells, he tells us, "drummed upon the hull of the plane as upon a drum. They pierced my fuel tanks. They might have drummed upon our bellies. . . . But who cares what happens to his body? Extraordinary how little the body matters." He goes on to describe an exhilarating non-attachment, a lack of concern for his personal safety or survival:

> Your son is in a burning house. Nobody can hold you back. You may burn up but do you think of that? You are ready to bequeath the rags of your body to any man who will take them.

The body doesn't matter because "Man is a knot, a web, a mesh into which relationships are tied. Only those relationships matter. The body is an old crock that nobody will miss" (105-7).

At first glance, Saint-Exupéry's account seems to have little in common with the story about the Polish mothers. The pilot experiences an elated self-abandonment, rushing headlong, like the boy's father, careless of consequences, vigorously active. By contrast, the mothers are victims, powerless and with no chance of escape. He survives to tell his story; the mothers do not. His voice speaks with authority; their voices are silenced. We know his name; they are anonymous. He loses nothing; they lose everything. The man rushes into the fire to bring back his son; the mothers attempting to save their children have them taken away.

Yet these opposites do not entirely exclude one another. Saint-Exupéry is vulnerable before the high-powered weapons, as he realizes, and the mothers take action despite their powerlessness. In both cases separation is accompanied by intuitions of interrelationship, and in both, self-surrender does not preclude engagement but transforms it through love and courage.

And yet, any suggestion that there is a comforting moral lesson in either of these stories should make us hesitate. The bravado of the fighter pilot is too close to cliché — the self-immolating ecstasy of a warrior bound for glory and the "ultimate sacrifice." And the mothers' horror is somehow cheapened by the suggestion that their story has a palliative dimension. We need to be careful, if only because there is no way to calculate or map the interplay, here, among non-attachment, suffering, compassion, liberation, tragedy, and redemption. The actual entanglements encompass and humiliate the theories by which we attempt to explain them. And so, although a moral teaching might well be clear and true, how it applies to the quicksands of our ordinary human confusions is another matter, calling for compassionate understanding rather than principle alone. Consequently, the Buddha's highly principled core teachings about non-attachment do not tell us the whole story.

The Buddha himself knew this, as we can see especially in the Discourses — the largest section of the Pali Canon of Buddhist scriptures. As we might expect, the Discourses are well supplied with straightforward declarations of the basic teachings — the Four Noble Truths, the Noble Eightfold Path, and so on. Also, the Buddha assures us that he intends to speak plainly: "The Dhamma well proclaimed by me thus is clear, open, evident and free of patchwork" (MD, 235). In the spirit of those words, he repeats the key point: "Both formerly and now what I teach is suffering and the cessation of suffering" (MD, 234). "Therefore," he tells the monks, "whatever is not yours abandon it," and as examples of what they should abandon he includes the body, feeling, perception, and consciousness. He insists also that each person is responsible for putting these instructions into action: "You should live as islands unto yourselves, being your own refuge, with no one else as your refuge." Austere advice, which might well encourage a similarly austere asceticism. Yet, as we know from his biography (or, more accurately, what tradition tells us about him), when the Buddha left his privileged palace world at age twenty-nine, he initially sought enlightenment through extreme ascetic practices, but after six years he concluded that he was getting nowhere, and took measures to attend to his physical well-being. On the one hand, the palace was too luxurious; on the other, asceticism was too destructive. The Buddha concluded that there must be a middle way, and by following it he attained enlightenment.

With the middle way in mind, we can now reconsider the austere core teachings which, as the Buddha knew, are not the whole story. And so there runs through the Pali Canon another strand, counterbalancing the Buddha's plainly declared doctrines. Although we need to be individually responsible, we should also understand that we are bound up with one another by way of a vast network of causes and effects. Consequently, the suffering of one is also the suffering of all. As the Bodhisattva ideal would later proclaim, none of us is liberated from suffering until all suffering ends. This sense of "interbeing," as the Vietnamese Buddhist writer Thich Nhat Hanh calls it, does not preclude people being their "own refuge," but complicates the process and in so doing allows the Buddha's teachings to engage with the lives of actual human beings, riven by imperfection and confused by all manner of desires, frustrations, hopes, and fears. Thus, although the Buddha sees human history as a catalogue of cravings, a nightmare sustained and driven by greed, hatred, and delusion, he nonetheless engages with a wide range of individual people, skillfully adjusting his teachings to their needs and capacities. After all, when he attained enlightenment there was no need for him to impart his perfect wisdom to others, and at first he thought he would not do so. The god Brahma is said to have persuaded him otherwise. And so the detachment of the enlightened sage and engagement with actual people in an imperfect world are maintained in a subtle yet powerful dialogical relationship — another version of the middle way, which best represents Buddhism's true genius.

We can understand something of how the Buddha thinks about the deep interconnectedness of "interbeing" by considering briefly the concepts of *karma* (*kamma* in Pali) and Dependent Origination (*paticca samupaddha*). *Kamma* is based on the idea that our actions are meritorious or culpable and that they set down memory traces predisposing us to similar kinds of behaviour in the future. When we die, our *kammic* history — our untamed desires, un-surrendered illusions, self-regarding behaviours and habits — continue, and are re-manifested in the world. Our "self" does not endure (it has no substantive existence); rather, the bundle of *kammic* patterns re-enters history, rather as a wave, which has a particular, transient identity, is neither the same as nor different from the ocean itself (and, of course, all the other waves).

The Chain of Dependent Origination describes how, in our unliberated condition, we are repeatedly bound back into suffering by the remanifestation ("rebirth") of our *kammic* history. The chain (which in detailed descriptions usually has twelve links) describes how birth and rebirth are conditioned by a clinging to desire, thereby giving rise to a new consciousness which takes on physical form, enthralling us once more with the promise of gratification, which we come, once more, to crave. The ocean of suffering in which we are immersed is thus a consequence of the vast *kammic* prehistory of our imperfections, which the ideal of a perfect liberation enables us to understand all the more clearly.

Again, however, *kamma* and Dependent Origination are ideas, and we need to turn to the Buddha's actual practice in the Discourses to show how skilfully the enlightened one brings these abstract teachings to bear in his dealings with imperfect people in an imperfect, *kamma*-burdened world. This engagement can hold some surprises for those who might be used to the idea of the Buddha in contemplation, serenely seated and half-smilingly benevolent. The Buddha of the Discourses can be a good deal more disconcerting.

For instance, in the *Ambattha Sutta,* the Buddha is confronted by a young man, Ambattha, who is a pupil of the Brahmin Pukkharasati. Ambattha visits the Buddha to question him, but is overbearing and arrogant, attacking the Buddha "with curses and insults." At last, the Buddha decides he has had enough and replies to Ambattha by first setting out the standard classification of the four main castes within Hinduism. These would be familiar to Ambattha, the disciple of a Hindu Brahmin. The Buddha then announces that Ambattha ought not to have such a head about himself because he is — though he does not know it — descended from a slave girl. Ambattha is astonished to hear the Buddha talk like this and does not know what to say. But the Buddha pursues him relentlessly: "If you don't answer, or evade the issue, if you keep silent or go away, your head will split in seven pieces" (LD, 115). The Buddha then summons a demon, who appears with "a huge iron club, ablaze and glowing, up in the sky just above Ambattha" (116). The young man is terrified, and the Buddha relents: "I must get him out of this," which he does by telling a parable to show that caste is unimportant for attaining enlightenment.

The chastened Ambattha returns to his Brahmin teacher, who is furious when he learns that the Buddha has been insulted. The Brahmin becomes "so angry and enraged that he kicked Ambattha over" (123) before heading off himself to visit the Buddha to make amends. When he arrives, the Buddha offers him a "graduated discourse" because his "mind was ready" (124), and the Brahmin becomes a lay disciple.

Throughout the *Ambattha Sutta,* the Buddha's language is carefully gauged to suit the mentality of his interlocutors. In response to the young man, the Buddha becomes aggressive, playing Ambattha at his own game. Then he turns to comically burlesque exaggeration, culminating in the theatrical business of the demon, neatly reversing Ambattha's aggressiveness. Finally, when the Buddha perceives that Ambattha needs reassuring, he turns the conversation in another direction, pointing out that caste is not important to enlightenment. By contrast, the Brahmin's "mind was ready," and the Buddha deals with him differently from the arrogant and juvenile disciple, who, as we see, is managed with a combination of verve and tough humour. Ambattha learns a lesson appropriate to his ability to receive it, as does the Brahmin. And so the Buddha engages these imperfect people imaginatively and by way of a discernment that can be, as circumstances require, energetic, humorous, and bracing. For the transmission of an authentic Buddhism, this combination of compassionate understanding and discernment is as important as the core teachings themselves.

What, then, about the self-sacrificing pilot freed from concern about his body and the mothers surrendering their babies? As we have seen, there is no lesson to be learned allowing us a clear route to despair or comfort. Rather, we might feel the protest against injustice that arises from the tragedy of suffering and also, from within that protest, an affirmation of compassion. These elements are woven together as complexly as we all are with one another. And so, when the Buddha learns about the good King Pasenadi's defeat in a battle against King Ajatasattu, he pauses first to notice the apparent injustice, the tragic unfairness of the world. After all, Ajatasattu is supported by evil friends and companions, and Pasenadi by good ones. It is no wonder that Pasenadi will sleep badly tonight. But the Buddha concludes on a different note:

> Victory breeds enmity,
> The defeated one sleeps badly.
> The peaceful one sleeps at ease,
> Having abandoned victory and defeat.
>   (CD, 177)

Elsewhere, the Buddha considers the condition of "a certain woman" whose children have died. Grieving, she wanders from street to street, asking for their whereabouts. The Buddha reflects: "And it can also be understood from this how sorrow, lamentation, pain, grief and despair are born from those who are dear, arise from those who are dear" (MD, 720). Attachment, it seems, whether to victory or defeat or to sons and daughters, brings sorrow, but the Buddha's tone is elegiac. He does not reprove; rather, he acknowledges the pain of our imperfect condition, and out of the centre of this understanding, compassion continues to offer its own, relentless protest.

7

Not So Good News
The Gospel According to Mark

Like the Buddha, whose Discourses were the main topic of the previous chapter, Jesus also taught by indirection, through parables and stories that engage people's imperfect understanding of his message about the Kingdom and how it can be attained. The most difficult aspect of this message is that it entails Jesus's crucifixion, the prelude to his resurrection and glorification in heaven. Jesus tells his followers, "Be ye therefore perfect, even as your Father which is in heaven is perfect" (Matt. 5:48), but he assures his disciples also that the way to perfection lies through suffering. This is so because of the imperfections of the world — the tragedy of history — and the Cross remains the sign of human cruelty and injustice that must be stopped because such things are an offense against God. But the message of the Cross is strong medicine, too strong even for Jesus's closest disciples, who insist on misunderstanding it. I want now to consider briefly some of the complex indirections by which the Gospel of Mark deals with the problem of accepting Jesus's crucifixion and the tragic view of the world that accompanies it.

The gospels first of all proclaim the "good news" (that is what "gospel," or "euangelion" means). Certainly, it is heartening to learn that Jesus came back from the dead and in so doing defeats death on our behalf. This mystical Christ — the crucified and resurrected redeemer — is pretty much invented by the pugnacious and gifted Paul, founder of Christianity as we know it. In turn, Paul's interpretation is imprinted on the gospels of Mark, Matthew, and Luke, the so-called "synoptic" gospels, meaning that they see the story with a single eye; through a single lens, as it were. John's gospel draws on a separate tradition, but all four evangelists agree in proclaiming Jesus's resurrection and the promise of a blessed reward beyond the pains of our mortal existence — for those who believe, that is, and whom God chooses.

As for the resurrected Jesus himself, well, he suffered abominably beforehand, and we are to understand that the righteous here and now can expect to suffer in a similar fashion, following him on the way of the Cross. And so it seems that the God who wants us to be restored to life, health, and community also permits dreadful suffering even to those closest to him.

One way to ease the weight of this difficult realization is to imagine Christ's glorious return at the end times, a mythical future in which a perfectly happy ending comes to pass. Meanwhile, the difficult realization continues to hold at the centre of our actual experience of God's management of our deeply imperfect human history, and I will want to say that the gospels remain compelling because they communicate so powerfully the tragic sense of life which this difficult realization entails. In short, if there is good news here, it is bittersweet, like tragedy.

Today, Mark's gospel is by and large accepted as the earliest, but it is impossible to be certain when or where or by whom any of the gospels was written. Abundant scholarly arguments serve mainly to highlight what we don't know, as a vast theoretical proliferation throws a smokescreen round an actual dearth of information. Yet, from internal evidence (gained, that is, by comparing the texts to one another), it seems likely that Matthew and Luke worked from Mark's prototype, developing his story with traditions of their own and, some say, a further shared source, now lost. In so doing, Matthew and Luke smooth over uncomfortable or cryptic passages in the craggy, alarmed, and rough-hewn Mark, at times airbrushing Mark's Jesus to conceal embarrassing details. For this reason alone, it seems unlikely that Mark's account would come after Matthew and Luke's. Also, it is inviting to see Mark's vivid and at times unflattered Jesus as somehow especially close to the original.

From the start, Mark draws our attention quite literally to the bittersweet. In Chapter 1, John baptizes Jesus in the river Jordan, and we are told that John eats locusts and wild honey. This is an odd detail, except that locusts are bitter and honey is sweet, and so John is caught up from the start in the difficult truth imparted by the narrative as a whole. This same juxtaposition continues through the opening chapter. The voice from heaven declares itself "well pleased" with Jesus, who is promptly driven "into the wilderness" (1:12). There he is threatened by "wild beasts" but is tended by "angels" (1:13). Divine glory — the voice from heaven and the angels — thus descends upon Jesus, who nonetheless wanders alone, under imminent threat of being eaten alive. By and by, in the crucifixion the wild (human) beasts will devour him in their own way, but we are assured (the good news again) that this too fulfills the divine plan.

We might at least admire the sheer, counterintuitive effrontery of the claim that the atrocity of Jesus's crucifixion can be a good thing, God's way of bringing us to glory. Yet, for their part, the disciples did not rush to accept such an assessment but fled the scene early. After all, the Romans crucified political dissidents wholesale, and Jesus's followers had good reason to fear. Afterwards, when the dead Jesus would not lie down, as it were, and when the ecstatic, formidable Paul had all but deified the mystical, resurrected Christ

(Paul never says straight out that Jesus was God), the early Christian churches needed to explain the disciples' failure of nerve, and why they did not fully realize what was going on. The bold proposal made by the churches is that the disciples' desertion of their wonder-working, charismatic leader was, in a sense, permitted by him because he did not fully let them in on the secret of his true identity. And so, in explaining the debacle of the crucifixion and the desertion of Jesus's runaway friends, the early churches had to develop a theory about when Jesus's messianic identity became evident: when, exactly, the Christological moment occurred. One result is that the gospels are a kind of literature like no other in the ancient world. They were, after all, developed for a highly specific, entirely unprecedented purpose.

For the authors of the gospels, that is, Jesus was the Christ, the Messiah come to proclaim the good news and to bring to glory those who believe in him. These things were proclaimed as facts, without any consideration that Jesus might not have thought of himself in such terms. Subsequently, through the centuries of Christendom, the gospel truth remained just that, but when secularism and skeptical enquiry permitted new freedoms of unbelief, alternative ways of looking at the historical Jesus also found new, persuasive advocates. In the nineteenth century, the so-called "life of Jesus" research was intrigued by the notion that the actual, historical Jesus and the Jesus of the gospels might not be quite identical. One influential book reflecting this kind of enquiry was written in 1901 by William Wrede, entitled *The Messianic Secret*.

In the present context, Wrede is interesting because the way he interprets Jesus's identity is opposite to that of the gospels. That is, he assumes that Jesus did not think of himself as the Messiah, and when the early churches wanted to declare otherwise, they proposed that Jesus had kept his identity secret. The disciples were therefore more or less in the dark until the resurrection caused them to see the light and the whole story became clear retrospectively. But why would Jesus do this? The gospels suggest that there were prudential reasons.

He would not want to provoke the authorities — Jewish or Roman — and he did not want the crowds to become even more pressing and unmanageable. Also, he did not want his disciples to make premature judgments about what kind of Messiah he was.

By contrast, Wrede's argument has the advantage of simplicity: the messianic claim was a secret because Jesus did not make it. Recent studies, such as those by Geza Vermes and the biography of Jesus by A.N. Wilson basically agree that Jesus was a Jewish *hasid,* or holy man, who preached to his people to encourage them to be better Jews. He did not think of himself as Christ the redeemer as proclaimed by Paul. For what it is worth, this view seems probable to me, but there is no way to be sure. Yet it is clear that Mark understood things differently, and we see this in how he deals with the secrecy motif.

When Jesus cures the leper (1:44), he tells the man to "say nothing," but the leper can't restrain himself and Jesus has to go into the desert to avoid the crowds. When Jairus's dead daughter is brought back to life, Jesus "charged them straitly that no man should know it" (5:43). The cured deaf-mute is also sworn to silence, but the news gets about anyhow (7:36). When the blind man at Bethsaida has his sight restored, Jesus tells him to keep quiet about it (8:26), and shortly after, when Peter suddenly twigs on and says, "Thou art the Christ," Jesus again says that the disciples "should tell no man of him" (8:30). When John, Peter, and James witness Jesus's transfiguration he tells them once more, as they come down the mountain, that they should "tell no man" until "the Son of man were risen from the dead" (9:9). But the disciples don't know what he is talking about, and at the foot of the mountain they try to cure a child afflicted by an evil spirit, but they can't do it, and Jesus performs the cure himself. He then discusses the matter with them, and, again, "he would not that any man should know it" (9:30).

Mark's emphasis on secrecy makes it hard not to think he has some further purpose in mind than merely to notice Jesus's concern not to be mobbed. After all, most of the injunctions to secrecy don't mention the crowds, though some do. Also, the injunctions them-selves are sometimes distinctly odd. Could the cured deaf-mute be expected not to tell anyone? What is Jairus to say about his dead daughter coming back to life? In general, the miracles can't be kept secret because they are public events, small examples of the kingdom of heaven breaking in among us, moments of "realized eschatology," as the theologians say. Yet Jesus insists. Why?

Part of the answer lies in the relationship between the miracle secrets and the messianic secret to which they point, and which Jesus is also anxious to preserve. Thus, he doesn't want Peter to put it about that Jesus is the Christ until after the resurrection. Again, this might be a prudent caution not to cause alarm among the authorities, who would not welcome the idea of a self-proclaimed messiah on the loose and perhaps ready to foment political unrest. But there is a further, more pressing reason, which becomes evident in the rhetorical strategy of Mark's entire gospel as it addresses the embarrassing fact that Jesus's followers deserted him at (literally) the crucial moment.

As I have suggested, the miracle secret and the messianic secret are interconnected. We might notice also that the miracles always occur as the result of faith and are not performed so that the afflicted might subsequently believe. Faith comes first; those who are cured have already acknowledged Jesus's special status, and the (outer) mir-acle cure is the symbol of an (inner) spiritual transformation: "Thy faith has made thee whole" (5:34), as Jesus says to the woman cured of the issue of blood.

The healing of the man sick of the palsy, who is lowered through the roof to gain access to Jesus, confirms this point. Jesus forgives the man's sins first, and only when the inner transformation is effected does Jesus cure the disease (2:10). Yet this story is so much at odds with the secrecy motif that we might wonder what is going on. Jesus deliberately provokes the scribes (2:6) and identifies himself as the "Son of man" (2:10) who has power to forgive sins. If the idea is to avoid dangerous publicity, this story has a dramatically opposite

72

effect. But avoiding dangerous publicity is never the main concern: rather, as I have noticed, the miracle stories point us to the messianic secret. And the reason the messianic secret needs to be kept is central to the entire design of Mark's gospel and to the kind of belief which it proclaims. Let us consider some elements of this design.

The cure of the blind man at Bethsaida is unique in the New Testament because Jesus at first doesn't get the cure quite right and has to try a second time. At first, he spits on the blind man's eyes and partly restores his sight ("I see men as trees, walking" [8:24] says the man, with touching eloquence). Jesus then has another try, and the man sees clearly.

This two-stage miracle occurs only in Mark. Matthew and Luke were uncomfortable with the suggestion of Jesus's fallibility, which they discreetly omit. But in so doing, they might also have missed Mark's point, which emerges when we read the story in context. Directly following upon the two-stage cure, Jesus asks the disciples, "Whom do men say that I am?" (8:27), and Peter replies, "Thou art the Christ" (2:29). Jesus then says that he, the Son of man, will suffer and be killed and will rise again. Peter doesn't like what he hears, and says so. Jesus promptly backhands him with a rebuke, severe to the point of intemperance: "Get thee behind me, Satan" (8:33).

Immediately following this episode, Peter, James, and John witness Jesus transfigured on the mountain, and as they descend, Jesus tells them again that the Son of man will have to suffer and will rise from the dead (9:9-12). The disciples aren't sure what he means (9:10), and when they get to the foot of the mountain they try to cure the child with the "dumb spirit," but they can't. Jesus reproves their lack of faith, and performs the cure himself, upon which the child's father utters the unforgettable words: "Lord, I believe; help thou mine unbelief" (9:24).

These stories are best read as a single unit. That is, the half-cured blind man corresponds to the half-insightful Peter who recognizes Christ but balks at the idea of suffering. Peter will need to achieve some further insight, as will the disciples who see Jesus transfigured but who, again, do not understand his message about suffering and resurrection. Not surprisingly, these half-awake disciples can't cure the child, and Jesus specifically says that their lack of faith is the problem. The child's father does better, and his haunting words reflect back directly on the disciples. "Lord, I believe: help thou mine unbelief" describes their own unsteady, half-insightful faith. But the child's father acknowledges his own imperfection, and in the man's wrestling with unbelief Jesus detects a saving honesty, and the miracle occurs. As always, faith begets miracles; not the reverse.

And so it now becomes clear what the secret really is about. It is not about the crowds, provocation, or, even, about the identity of the Son of man. It is about the one thing the disciples don't want to accept, namely, the Cross. As we see, Peter objects, the disciples don't understand, and so Jesus says, basically, keep quiet about this whole thing until you see what is going to happen, for at the present moment you are half blind. In theological language, the Cross is necessary for an adequate Christology, but the disciples cannot accept this difficult realization, this bitter part of the Lord's message. Jesus of course does go on to suffer, and only at the resurrection does the meaning of his death become clear. The resurrection, then, is the final miracle secret that reveals the messianic secret in all its unbearable, paradoxical grandeur.

Rather than offer a palliative cure for the problem of suffering, Mark's gospel proclaims the problem itself as the fact against which belief is most likely to break. The best of men endures the worst suffering; that is the way of the world, and in the name of everything good, a conscionable person will recoil in protest. Out of that resistance, for some there is faith, rooted in a demand and expectation that the way of the world will not prevail. For believers, a radical transformation has been effected already within history, and we await its completion in Christ's second coming. For the rest of us, the enduring power of the gospel lies not so much in this promise as in the disturbing effectiveness with which it communicates a tragic sense of life, holding a mirror up to the nature of our

actual bittersweet predicament, sustained by ideas of perfect righteousness and liberation while living in a violent, imperfect world.
Yet the bittersweet is also life-enhancing, as tragedy is, offering an
astringent truth that reveals us to one another in our strength and
frailty, our infinite aspirations and difficult, sometimes glorious,
impermanence.

PART II *Self*

8

Immortal Souls and State Executions

As I am attempting to suggest throughout these essays, the sense we have of ourselves as individual moral agents is closely bound up with our ideals. That is, by aspiring to some (perfect) ideal and falling short, we become aware of our imperfections, which in turn might cause us to feel guilty and irresponsible. In this case, the stability of the self and its enduring identity over time is assumed: if a person is responsible for actions committed in the past, there must be some substantive, continuing identity between that person then and now. In short, the more strongly one feels guilt, the more sharply defined is the self as a bearer of responsibilities.

Judaism, Christianity, and Islam share a common insistence on the idea that human beings are responsible before the all-seeing, perfect God who will judge each of us individually, consigning the enduring self (which remains self-identical after death) to an eternity of bliss or torment. The usefulness of this idea is that it asserts the immense, incalculable significance of moral action and of the self as a moral agent. The downside is that guilt and its attendant anxieties can be harmful, not least because they can so readily be projected onto scapegoats. Likewise, responsibility can be interpreted as requiring, or even forcing, others to accept the One God whose impending judgment we all alike should fear.

Vindictive self-righteousness is, therefore, one unfortunate liability of an exaggerated view of the stability and enduring identity of the self and its assumption of responsibilities that have eternal consequences. But, as a moment's reflection makes clear, the self also is unstable, volatile, and often fragmented. The changes that can occur to a person over time can be on the order of a virtual metamorphosis. Yet pushing this point too far also leads to absurdities, because if there were no continuity whatsoever, we could not act purposefully, even in performing the simplest tasks. The challenge is therefore to balance the fact that, on the one hand, our ideas about perfection awaken us to imperfections for which we need to assume responsibility, striving to do better, and, on the other hand, that our imperfections and uncertain self-identity are simply part of what we are — unstable creatures emerging into more or less adequate ways of knowing: fragile, volatile, and needing our mutual insecurities to help us get along without resorting to ego-inflated self-righteousness or callous indifference.

With these points in mind, I would like to consider two examples in which the interpretation of responsibility in relation to self-identity is, literally, a matter of life and death. These examples are executions conducted in the United States by two governors who would later become president.

In February 1998, in a jail in Huntsville, Texas, Karla Faye Tucker was executed by lethal injection. In 1983, Karla had murdered two people with a pickaxe. The circumstances were a routinely sordid mix of drugs, biker gangs, theft, and intimidation. Karla was twenty-three at the time, but by age twelve she already had a drug problem. At thirteen she ran off with a rock band, and later took up with bikers and did a stint as a prostitute. She claimed that when she was strik-ing the pickaxe into her victims, she had orgasms. The jury scarcely hesitated in recommending that she be executed.

During her fourteen years on death row, Karla found Jesus. She became involved in the prison ministry and even married the chap-lain. (At the ceremony, bride and groom were separated by an acrylic partition.) As the date of her execution neared, Karla requested that her death sentence be commuted to life imprisonment. An unlikely assortment of influential people and agencies pleaded on her behalf. These included Pope John Paul II, the World Council of Churches, the UN Commissioner Bacre Waly Ndiaye, the Italian Prime Minis-ter Romano Prodi, and even those hang-'em-high stalwarts from the US religious right, Jerry Falwell and Pat Robertson. Predictably, the media cashed in on the predicament of an agreeably good-looking and still youngish enough woman imminently to be tied down and lethally penetrated. Would mercy prevail, sparing her the ordeal, or would the law have its way?

Meanwhile, Karla remained candid, articulate, and un-self-pity-ing, even if a tad starry-eyed. TV interviews revealed her as her own most credible witness to the fact that, whatever she had done in the past, she had now changed. Even the Texas prosecutor, Charley Davidson, who had secured the death penalty for Karla's accomplice, Danny Garrett, intervened on her behalf. (Danny died in jail from liver failure before his executioners could get to him.) Karla was now "a completely different person," the prosecutor said, not the same at all as the killer of Jerry Lynn Dean and Deborah Thornton: "That person no longer exists." Charley wasn't quite right about this, but the adversarial world to which he was habituated would best hear things straight-up, and Charley had his point to make.

In the end, it lay with the state governor to decide whether or not to recommend a stay of execution. But George W. Bush was at that time running the most active death chamber in any US state in recent history. Governor Bush sought "guidance through prayer" before going on to deny clemency (as they say). In his autobiography he confides that the decision imposed a heavy burden on him. Yet his self-portrayal as a pained but piously dutiful servant of the law is shown in a different light by a conversation which took place the next year, in 1999, recorded by the conservative reporter Tucker Carlson. When Carlson asked Bush about Karla's appeal, the governor pursed his lips in imitation of a little girl pleading and then mock-whimpered, "Please don't kill me." The not-especially-sensitive Carlson admits to being shocked.

In 1981, in Conway, Arkansas, while attempting to commit a robbery, Ricky Ray Rector fatally shot a policeman and a bystander. Ricky Ray then put the gun to his own head, but in firing a bullet into his skull he managed only to render himself irreparably brain-damaged. He was subsequently tried and condemned to die, like Karla, by lethal injection.

Ricky Ray seems not to have understood his predicament, not least because he was heavily medicated to prevent his already insulted brain from pitching him into intolerable psychotic delusions. When given a last meal before his execution, he put the pecan pie dessert aside, saying that he wanted to save it "for later."

But if Ricky Ray didn't know what was up, the governor had a clearer view of the rights and wrongs of the matter. Like George Bush, Bill Clinton was keen that justice be done, and he was keen also not to be seen as soft on crime. In the previous bid for the presidency by a Democrat, Michael Dukakis had foundered on just this issue, and, as ever, Clinton was a quick study. Just days before the New Hampshire primary election, he left the campaign trail and hurried to Arkansas to preside in person over Ricky Ray's execution.

As it happens, Ricky Ray's antipsychotic medication made it difficult for the ministering officials to find a suitable vein. They sliced at his limbs behind a screen so that observers couldn't see the mess, though they heard Ricky Ray groaning in distress as he also, pathetically, tried to help the procedure along. Eventually, the team of two "medical" personnel was increased to five so that they could work on both sides of Ricky Ray's body, performing "cut-downs" in search of a route to his heart. At last they found their way, and put him to sleep.

As with Karla's defenders, so with Ricky Ray's, the main argument claimed that he was no longer sufficiently the same person who had committed the crime. As we see, in neither case did this argument prevail, and the person who committed the crime yesterday was held to be essentially the same person who remained responsible today and who would be executed tomorrow.

For eminently practical purposes, of course, we rely all the time on the commonsensical assumption that personal identity is relatively stable. I expect my wife to be recognizably the same person today as yesterday, and if someone should behave like a series of very different people from one day to another, we might correctly consider that an illness. In one sense, Karla Faye and Ricky Ray were indeed the same people who committed the crimes, and yet, in another, non-trivial, sense they were not.

As I have suggested, in the Abrahamic faith traditions especially, individual choice, responsibility, and personal accountability before God are vehemently insisted upon. Partly in consequence, Christianity invented a hell of eternal torment for those whose immortal souls are judged culpable by the All-Merciful, who can be counted on to stick to principles and not to shrink from condemning even his beloved creatures to a capital punishment of never-ending duration. Not surprisingly, secularized (or semi-secularized) versions of this broad understanding of divine justice are likely to insist also on an essential, enduring self — or "soul"— which is the bearer of responsibilities over time. The prayerful Bush was therefore merely tuning himself in to a set of pre-understandings by means of which the religious and secular move along in harmony, like a gracious waltzing couple.

Most notably among the world's other main religions, Buddhism argues firmly against the idea of a substantive self, and Buddhism has been an effective ally of Western philosophers, cultural critics, and others whose efforts, especially since the second half of the twentieth century, are committed to providing a critique of totalitarianisms, imperialist self-righteousness, authoritarian certitudes, and the like. Put simply, the Buddha argues that we have no soul in the sense of a substantive entity that endures during our life and survives our death. Rather, human personality is a provisional unity of different physiological and psychological elements or "aggregates," more or less stable according to circumstances, and capable of making moral choices — not the least of which is surrendering a desire for personal immortality.

Among Western philosophers, David Hume in the eighteenth century made similar arguments against the independent existence of a substantive self, and among twentieth-century philosophers in the Humean line, Derek Parfit (*Reasons and Persons,* corrected ed. [Oxford: Clarendon, 1987]) links Hume's conclusions to the Buddha's and maintains that the Buddha was right about the soul (though Parfit's Buddhist critics scold him for putting his own twist on what the Buddha actually said).

Basically, Parfit argues for the quite modest proposal that we are not separately existing entities "apart from our brains and bodies, and various interrelated physical and mental events" (216). Persons do indeed exist as thinkers and agents with complex lives and relationships. But there is no essence or soul or "deep further fact" separate from the thoughts, actions, experiences, and relationships making up the life of the individual in question, whose identity is not fixed and immutable, but indeterminate and capable of change. Of course, there is continuity: Karla was once a child, and there is a physical and psychological connectedness all the way back. But in 1998, Karla was no longer that child, any more than a sunflower seed is the sunflower. As Parfit says, our identity is like a rope, no single strand of which is continuous along the entire length; just so, our connections to our past and future selves are a complex interlacement of overlapping elements. Consequently, we are not so much self-identical individuals as provisionally stable amalgams of psycho-physical effects, values, beliefs, goals, and habits. Parfit cites Hume in suggesting that persons have the same kind of unity as does a nation or commonwealth — such entities exist, but no under-lying essence survives when they are dismantled. Likewise, human persons do not have an independently existing soul, and although we might wish for more, the fact is, we do not know what happens to us after we die, and we tell ourselves stories about an afterlife to provide purpose and stability in an imperfect world where there is much suffering and injustice and where we are all at last condemned to perish.

Yet, in general, people are reluctant to surrender belief in some form of the "deep further fact," and even in Buddhist countries an uncomfortable gap typically exists between a learned elite who pro-pound the austere doctrine of "no soul" (*anatta*) and the practitioners of a popular Buddhism who resort to ceremony, prayer, and a myriad of observances to ensure a good rebirth, imagined as personal sur-vival, an antidote to anxiety about the prospect of non-existence. But, again like the Buddha, Parfit has found that a surrender of the "deep further fact" can be liberating rather than a cause of despair:

> When I changed my view, the walls of my glass tunnel disappeared. I now live in the open air. There is still a difference between my life and the lives of other people. But the difference is less. Other people are closer. I am less concerned about the rest of my own life, and more concerned about the lives of others. (281)

The key to Parfit's finding himself "more concerned" is his experi-ence of the self as having flexible boundaries. Because this is so, we do not act merely as individuals, out of self-interest; rather, our moral lives are closely bound up with one another, and even after we die, the consequences of our actions live on. For instance, decisions we might make in our professional lives about jobs, housing, ecology, social welfare, and so forth, can affect future generations. Such deci-sions might even determine whether or not people are born, because social policy might create circumstances within which families can or cannot thrive.

In short, because boundaries between selves are marked by strong or weak kinds of continuity, we are deeply interrelated as moral agents. By contrast, the theory that we act mainly out of self-interest places heavy stress on our separateness as persons and, consequently, underplays the significance of what we do together (443). Far from being nihilist, Parfit's non-religious theory of what it means to be a person encourages a compassionate involvement with others, and with this in mind we can return to the hapless Karla Faye and Ricky Ray.

As we see, Karla was rehabilitated, and not even her executioners disputed the fact that she had become a richer, more compassionate human being, a threat to no one. Ricky Ray also was changed, but he was less than he had been (rather than more, as in Karla's case), and no one disputed that he was brain-damaged and irreparably diminished in his capacities. Of course, the justice system in the United States (as elsewhere) recognizes that people do indeed change. Diminished responsibility, mitigating circumstances, rehabilitation, and early release for good behaviour are familiar currency in the assessment of culpability and punishment. Yet, despite such provisions, judgment remained firm on the assumption that Karla Faye and Ricky Ray were sufficiently the same as they had been and that they therefore remained wholly responsible.

Karla's last words were a promise, now that she was going to Jesus, that she would wait there to welcome her friends (including the warden). Ricky Ray (as we see) thought he was going to have his dessert later. In each case, I would want to suggest, the probability is about equal. Meanwhile, the prayerful Bush reassured anyone who cared to listen that "judgements about the heart and soul of an individual on death row are best left to a higher authority." That is, God alone knows the secrets of Karla's soul, and Bush humbly submits to God's higher judgment while getting on with the business of taking the life from her body. Leaving God's mercy to God alone while imitating God's vindictiveness affords a two-edged legitimation against which Karla Faye, Ricky Ray, and the nameless and innumerable multitude like them, have stood no chance at all.

The grand delusion here is that we can know in the first place about God's intimate concern for each of our immortal souls, or that we have the permission of a perfectly loving God to kill others. Some Christian theologians (for instance, the French Protestant Jacques Ellul and the Irish Catholic James Mackey), as well as many Christian believers across the denominations, refuse to justify the taking of human life in God's name. Yet the moral perceptions of such people are not shared by the more zealously vindictive among their Christian brethren who peruse the Good Book and readily enough find other ways to sow the seeds of God's love on earth.

Certainly, children playing in Baghdad and the Sudan had never heard of Karla Faye or Ricky Ray, any more than they had heard of cruise missiles. Like children anywhere, they probably for the most part looked forward to the adventure of growing up. They could not be expected to imagine how they would become the beneficiaries of yet another act of principled destruction, responsibly and righteously undertaken by the good governors who had put themselves to school in the death chambers of Texas and Arkansas before each, in his turn, became president of the one nation, under God.

9

The Eyes Have It
Seeing One's Self and Others

In this chapter, I want to consider how dominant theories about society and about personality mirror each other, so that the way we see others reflects how we see ourselves. Here, for instance, is Dante, greatest poet of the Middle Ages, looking into his beloved Beatrice's eyes in the third section of *The Divine Comedy*:

> As in a looking-glass a flame is caught,
>> A waxen torch behind us being lit,
>> Anticipating thus our sight and thought,
>
> And, glancing round to test the truth of it,
>> We find that glass and flame as well agree
>> As notes and melody together fit,

So, I remember, did it prove to be,
  While I was gazing in the lovely eyes
  Wherewith Love made a noose to capture me;

For, as I turned, there greeted mine likewise
  What all behold who contemplate aright
  That heaven's revolution through the skies.

One Point I saw, so radiantly bright,
  So searing to the eyes it strikes upon,
  They needs must close before such piercing light.

The "lovely eyes" are Beatrice's, and they have made him captive. But as the first two stanzas tell us, Dante does not look straight at Beatrice; rather, he sees her at an angle, so that his gaze is refracted and he catches a reflection of the heavenly glories above and behind him. Her eyes thus resemble a "looking-glass," and if he had gazed straight into them he would have seen only himself. Instead, he looks at an angle, and glimpses God's transcendent glory — the "One Point" so bright that it sears his eyes when he turns to look directly at it. And so, in and through Beatrice's eyes, Dante comes to see the divine source of love itself. All of which reproduces the theological idea that the whole of creation manifests God's design, and we should not love God's creatures — the things of this world — in and for themselves, but because they embody and participate in God's glory. To have gazed straight at Beatrice would have been idolatry, shutting out God, who would be replaced by Beatrice alone. By contrast, the divine light gives Beatrice an infinite value.

Another great poet — from the Renaissance, now, rather than the Middle Ages — was also much taken up with the idea of a lover looking into his mistress's eyes. But in John Donne, the lover looks directly at the lady, in whose eyes he sees his own image. Thus, in *The Good Morrow,* the speaker says that their eyes are hemispheres, together making up a complete world which excludes everyone but themselves. And in *The Exstasie* Donne develops this idea through a brilliant combination of high seriousness and ironic playfulness.

The Exstasie opens with a brief account of a May landscape. The speaker reminds his lover how, while reclining and holding hands on a bank covered with spring flowers, they had once fallen into a trance. He recalls how their souls had interpenetrated while their bodies lay side by side, inert. His explanation is a witty tour de force, as the speaker describes the relationships between soul and body, and the perplexing elusiveness and strangeness of the ecstatic condition. At last, he brings the narrative back to the present, saying what a relief it is to be back in the body, the material condition in which we are most ourselves, most human.

The speaker develops this argument with such dexterity that we are not sure at the end whether he wants mainly to praise the spiritual ecstasy or to recommend making love physically, as a relief from the strange complications of the ecstatic condition. The lady might well admire his high-mindedness and intelligence, but she (along with the reader) might also suspect his motives. Certainly, his bewitching seriousness keeps us guessing, or at least wrong-footed. Here are some lines from the beginning of the poem, where he describes how they lay side by side:

Our hands were firmely cimented
    With a fat balme, which thence did spring,
Our eye-beames twisted, and did thred
    Our eyes, upon one double string;

So to' entergraft our hands, as yet
    Was all our meanes to make us one,
And pictures on our eyes to get
    Was all our propagation.

As they gaze into one another's eyes, they see themselves reflected. That is what is meant by "And pictures in our eyes to get / Was all our propagation," which alludes to a contemporary saying, "to look babies" — that is, to see a small image of yourself reflected in someone else's eyes. In Latin, *pupilla* means "orphan" or "young person," and the diminutive, *pupa,* means "doll." And so, in the pupil of the other person's eye, you see a doll-like image of yourself. "Propagation" means that the lovers again beget their own images by looking at each other.

The lines about the eyebeams twisted on a "double string" also draw on an idea current in Donne's time, claiming that eyesight depends on a beam of light going out from the eye ("extramission") and on one coming in from the object ("intramission"). Conventionally, eyesight is the highest sense, the least material and most easily associated with spirit (illumination, enlightenment): thus, the eyes are the windows of the soul. And so, the fact that Donne's lovers gaze into one another's eyes is a fit prologue to their spiritual ecstasy.

But it is hard to miss how emphatically, indeed how almost grotesquely material Donne's language is. The eyebeams "thred" the eyes like beads on a string (or two strings, twisted). And when he describes their palms "firmely cimented / With a fast balme," he is telling her how their sweat is a glue that cements or bonds them together. In both cases the body entraps, and we are tangled by it and glued to its intense materiality. In contrast, the effortless, free communion of souls is a welcome escape, a liberation.

The poem then turns to the ecstatic condition, describing the union of souls and their identity in the disembodied state. But problems soon arise. If the souls do indeed interpenetrate perfectly, what is the difference between them, and how should this difference be described without reference to a body? Here is what the speaker says:

> This Extasie doth unperplex
>   (We said) and tell us what we love,
> We see by this, it was not sexe,
>   We see, we saw not what did move:
>
> But as all severall soules containe
>   Mixture of things, they know not what,
> Love, these mixt soules, doth mixe againe,
>   And makes both one, each this and that.

The promise of the first line, that the ecstasy clarifies ("doth unperplex"), is undermined by what follows as the argument swerves ingeniously through a perilous, complex course which is captivating but hardly unperplexing. "We see, we saw not what did move" sets the tone, as we find ourselves caught in a momentary hesitation, grasping for the sense. The souls are apparently mixed of "things," but "they know not what," and the mixed souls are then mixed again, so that the "this" and "that" are made one. Perhaps the speaker means that the highest (rational) soul contains the lower (animal and vegetable) souls, and by a process of refinement, or remixing, the spiritual part emerges and is able to enter into communion with another spirit, far superior to the mere physical union of ordinary lovers.

The speaker's sophistication and intelligence are clearly on show here, as he praises the transcendent value of spiritual communion. But a current of ironic humour also runs through these lines, as the slick, bewitching complexity ends up demonstrating that the ecstasy is, in its own way, just as problematic as the experience of being tangled and trapped in a material body. Consequently, as the poem moves to a conclusion, the speaker, with some relief, turns away from the ecstasy and back to the material world:

> But O alas, so long, so farre
>   Our bodies why do we forbeare?

But having spoken so highly of the ecstasy, the narrator must now make a commensurate case for the body, and there follows another dazzling passage on why we should be grateful to have our bodies, and to return to them.

The main debate among critics of this poem focuses on how seriously to take the praise of ecstasy. Is the poem a high-minded affirmation of spiritual communion after which the lovers return to ordinary life, or is it an ironic, playfully elaborate seduction, an attempt to get the lady to accept that physical love is best? The second alternative strikes me as the more convincing and more interesting, but I want to return briefly to the lovers looking into one another's eyes, and to notice how different Donne's poem is from Dante's.

As we see, in *The Exstasie* the lovers' eyes are described in a way that strongly polarizes the material and spiritual, a contrast that the rest of the poem develops. The peculiar imagery of statues, cement, and eyeballs on a string suggests that matter entraps spirit, but the spiritual ecstasy is also a little deranged in its perplexing liberation from the material realm. Here we might recall that Donne lived in the age of Bacon (1561–1626) and Descartes (1596–1650) — that is, the age of the modern scientific revolution, during which the study of material nature was effectively divorced from the study of theology and metaphysics. In short, Dante's vision of a universe in which all things mirror the design of the Creator, a design that could be read off by the appreciative human mind referring God's reflected glories back to the One Source, is now replaced by a world where the realm of extension (matter) and the realm of spirit (mind) are separate. By making this distinction, the new scientists could get on with studying the material world in and for itself. They could also of course be pious believers, but as scientists they did not explain the laws of the material world theologically, but mathematically and by way of experiment. Not surprisingly, this also is the age when the mind-body problem consumed the attention of philosophers — as we see, for instance, in Descartes, Locke, Leibniz, Spinoza, and Malebranche. Donne belongs in this company insofar as his poem also engages head-on with the difference between mind and body, spirit and matter, as well as their complex interactions. The lovers gazing at each other are, as it were, in their own world, their individuality constituting the uniqueness of their relationship, which remains informed by traditional religious values and understandings, however irreverently and ironically interpreted.

My final example is from Samuel Beckett, who, as it happens, admired Dante and was fascinated by the mind-body problem as

formulated by Descartes. In Beckett's novel *Murphy*, the title character compares himself to Belacqua, the inhabitant of Dante's
Purgatorio, canto 4, who is being punished for indolence. He has to
wait a period of time as long as his earthly life before being allowed
to climb the mountain of purgatory. Belacqua's awareness that
indolence is a sin is all the more powerfully brought home to him by
the fact that he has to wait, indolently, until his sentence is served
before he can even begin the labours that will release him. The poignant, agonizing fruitlessness of Belacqua's torpid but painfully
self-aware condition appealed to Beckett, who refers to Belacqua
again elsewhere.

The indolent, Belacqua-like Murphy lives in London, and with the
connivance of his landlady, he sponges off a rich uncle in Holland;
also, he has a relationship with a prostitute, Celia, who gets him to
propose to her. But if he and Celia are to live together, Murphy must
find work, and eventually he takes a job in a mental hospital, where
he soon feels at home among the inmates and decides to stay. He is
given a small room with a gas fire fed by a tap in the toilet, and he
strikes up a relationship with a Mr. Endon. In the end, Murphy gets
blown up in an accident with the gas fire.

At the beginning of the novel, we find Murphy seated on a chair
and attempting to put himself into a trance or ecstasy, a spiritual
condition that would separate his mind from his body so that out-
ward events would not affect him. He goes on seeking this ecstatic
condition throughout the novel, and thinks he comes closest to
achieving it in the asylum. Yet, he also needs some further human
relationship, as is evident in his regard for Celia and his concern for
Mr. Endon.

Murphy's situation can almost seem a parody not only of Dante's
Belacqua, but also of Donne's lover, who seeks likewise to escape
from his body but finds himself needing a physical human relationship. Here, now, is Beckett's version of the mutual gaze, as Murphy
looks in Mr. Endon's eyes, holding the man's face so close that their
foreheads almost touch:

> Approaching his eyes still nearer Murphy could see the red frills of
> mucus, a large point of suppuration at the root of an upper lash,
> the filigree of veins like the Lord's prayer on a toenail and in the
> cornea, horribly reduced, obscured and distorted, his own image.
> They were all set, Murphy and Mr. Endon, for a butterfly kiss, if
> that is still the correct expression. (249)

As with Donne's lovers, Murphy sees his own image reflected. The
difference is that Mr. Endon in return doesn't recognize Murphy at
all, and when they part, we are told, "The last Mr. Murphy saw of Mr.
Endon was Mr. Murphy unseen by Mr. Endon." Also, the close-up
shows the unappealing anatomy of Mr. Endon's eye, with its mucus
and suppuration, and Murphy notices how the cornea distorts and
reduces the reflection, so that he appears "horribly reduced, obscured
and distorted." The sentence on the butterfly kiss, then, is whimsi-
cal, drawing our attention to the highly unromantic reality of the
romantic motif of the mutual gaze. The comically painful close-
up gives Murphy only a disenchanted view of himself and of Mr.
Endon, and leaves Murphy with the deflating recognition that he is
utterly unrecognized. Clearly, this account of looking into the eyes
of another person for whom you care is quite different from Donne's dazzling poem with its energetic psychological engagement,
and from the Dantesque vision where the other person is most fully
recognized as a mirror of God's perfection. "This greatest master of
nothing," Harold Bloom calls Beckett, yet noticing also the "gusto"
with which Beckett communicates his anxiety-ridden nihilism. And
indeed Beckett redeems a poignant, wry compassion from the ashes
of the disenchantment he describes so remorselessly.

The modern theory of personality that perhaps best resonates
with the kind of anxiety and disenchantment we find in Beckett
is Freud's. For Freud, as for Beckett, personality is unstable, carried along by the force of habit and conditioned reflex, shaped by
unconscious drives and complexes, impeded by blocks, fuelled by
repression, riven by anxiety and emptied of traditional spiritual

content. This is not to say that Beckett is somehow "Freudian" but only that his work reflects the climate of the times, and the analogy with Freud can help us to see this. With this kind of analogy in mind, I have chosen my three examples because they are typical of certain dominant theories of personality and, correspondingly, of certain dominant ideological concerns of the cultures that produced them: the High Middle Ages, the High Renaissance, and High Modernism. In so doing, I have wanted to show that our view of somebody else is interwoven with what we think of ourselves and our place in the social order. That is, dominant theories about personality are reflected in and reproduce dominant ideas about society.

Still, there are limits to this correspondence. No doubt there was despair, futility, and emptiness in the thirteenth century, and not all modern people feel like an atom of consciousness adrift in an empty universe driven by arbitrary, unconscious forces. Also, the literature I have chosen provides its own reasons for having us pull back from an oversimplified view of a straightforward mirror imagery between self and society. Dante, Donne, and Beckett remain utterly distinctive. Although they are of their times, each is unmistakably himself, producing a poetry marked by a quality that can in the end only be recognized and affirmed. Analogously, the individual self is precisely that which also escapes definition, even as it goes on opening up new paths of communication and possibilities of relationship.

It seems, then, that persons occupy two positions simultaneously: the first is determined by the constraints imposed by history and society; the second opens upon the possibility for relationship and communication that escapes definition, struggling to reshape society from within history's constraints. On the one hand, to remove a person from the material and ideological circumstances of history merely reaffirms the unhelpful notion of a private, unitary self, which then makes the body all the more vulnerable to the controlling designs of the politically powerful. On the other hand, to deny the person a certain mystery represented by the possibilities of further, unpredictable kinds of communication is to deny the subjectivity without which it is, again, easy to reduce both self and other to material objects. In a social order that avoids these errors, the general good of society is the organization of particular goods offered and accepted by each person, who in turn is shaped and sustained, in however contingent a fashion, by the exchange itself. In looking into one another's eyes, Dante's, Donne's, and Beckett's characters explore something of this perpetually dynamic relationship between self and other, person and society, constraint and freedom. And to some degree we can see ourselves in each of them.

The God of Battles and the Irish Dimension
of Shakespeare's Henry V

In the previous chapter I considered the idea that personal identity is shaped by social norms and values and that the self is flexible, conflicted, and uncertainly emergent through relationship and dialogue. One further complication is that, especially in professional life, people typically present to the world a face they know is not identical with their private selves. The psychoanalyst Carl Gustav Jung used the term *persona* for this public aspect of the self. Thus, a person who is a soldier, banker, politician, lawyer, musician, doctor, and so on, will adopt a persona in order to behave in a manner conforming to the standards expected of the occupation in question. Not surprisingly, this persona conceals a more complex, underlying self, as, for instance, no end of supposedly scandalous revelations about the private lives of politicians continue to remind us. Nonetheless, identifying too strongly with the persona can also be dangerous because it invites ego-inflation and the repression of one's ordinary imperfections.

No one has examined the interrelationships between private self and public persona more probingly than William Shakespeare. This is so especially in his history plays, and here I want briefly to consider *Henry V,* which recounts the English victory over the French at the Battle of Agincourt in 1415.

The public persona of a king, such as Henry V, represents an extreme case of how a public role can shape an individual's sense of identity. Indeed, the king is supposed to become his persona, as the ancient conception of the king's two bodies indicates: "The king is dead, long live the king" means that the person next in line for the throne will not just step into the role, but will actually embody the divinely appointed royal institution itself. In turn, the king is said to embody his people, so that he represents them and also defines them as a group. The political scientist Frank Wright describes this as "representative identity," a term that has an interesting further dimension in addition to the sense exemplified by the king's royal persona. This further dimension occurs, as Wright explains, when a person who is identified as belonging to another group is taken to represent that group regardless of the person's actual opinions and allegiances. In the next chapter I will deal more fully with this further sense, but for now, I want simply to notice that representative identity in both senses is not one's real identity, nor is the persona one's actual self. No end of mischief ensues from confusions about this, as Shakespeare invites us to see in the story of Henry V's stirring military victory.

"God fought for us." These words — always disturbing — are spoken by Henry V after the Battle of Agincourt, as the king reflects on how a small, exhausted British army (Shakespeare goes out of his way to have Irish, Scots, and Welsh in it, as well as English) defeated a much superior French force. Mainly, the play celebrates Henry's stunning victory and the success of his collateral descendants, the Tudors — especially Elizabeth I, who ruled when *Henry V* was written in 1599. The result is Shakespeare's most jingoistic celebration of martial prowess, and it is worrisome, not least because Shakespeare, who knew everything, wrote it.

Also, there is an Irish dimension, which is significant because it pertains to the play's interest in the idea of identity — both Henry's and his followers'. This Irish dimension emerges most clearly in some remarkable lines spoken by the chorus, imagining Henry's return to England as a "conqu'ring Caesar" (5.Chorus.28). In much the same way, we are told, another, present-day conqueror might also return: "The general of our gracious empress / (As in good time he may) from Ireland coming / Bring rebellion broachèd on his sword" (5.Chorus.30–32). The "gracious empress" is Elizabeth, and the "general" is the Earl of Essex, who, in the same year as Shakespeare wrote the play, was dispatched to Ireland by the Queen to put down the rebellious Earl of Tyrone, Hugh O'Neill. But O'Neill was no pushover, and Essex soon found himself hard pressed. Against the Queen's wishes, he returned to London and, frantic, made his way into her bedroom. She promptly had him arrested.

Clearly, Shakespeare wrote the lines about "the general" before Essex's disgrace (they were dropped the following year, though they are printed in modern editions), and they show that the play is not just a compliment to the Tudors, but also an encouragement to Essex to do in Ireland the same thing as Henry did in France. Essex is to bring "rebellion broachèd on his sword" — spitted, that is, like meat for the grill — just as, at the siege of Harfleur, Henry warns the townspeople that "your naked infants" will be "spitted upon pikes" and your old men will have their "reverend heads dashed to the walls" (3.3.37–38). So you'd better surrender, Henry tells them, and no one doubts that he means it, just as he means it when he says, "God fought for us" (4.8.119). Like the French, the Irish also are the enemy, and it doesn't matter if old people and infants are killed, because they are representatives of the enemy as a whole. This convenient demonizing requires an equivalent, oversimplified righteousness on the part of the aggressors, and the king, God's representative, behaves accordingly, identifying himself with his own aggrandized persona, with God fighting for him, and with his cause, which is justified by England's highest ecclesiastical authorities.

There is a good deal about God in *Henry V,* and religion plays a part both in preparing for the invasion and in justifying it afterwards. At the start, the Archbishop of Canterbury and the Bishop of Ely answer Henry's question about whether or not he can "justly and religiously" (1.2.10) attack France. They deliver a long, tangled speech about genealogy and the history of Salic law, concluding that "as clear as is the summer's sun" (1.2.86), Henry's rights have been usurped. They then offer the king a "mighty sum" (1.2.133) of money to help finance the war, and we recollect that immediately before their meeting with Henry they had been worried about a law that might soon be passed in England, allowing the annexation of church property. On this topic, the bishops think that Henry might be wavering, and now they are concerned to win his favour. Consequently, their speech has to impress him by being learned and detailed, and yet they need to deliver a clear message telling the king what he wants to hear — clear as the summer sun.

For his part, Henry seems barely to listen to the long-winded, apparently scrupulous preamble. When it is over, he goes for the bottom line: "May I with right and conscience make this claim?" (1.2.96). The Bishops give him his answer, and so God gets brought in, along with the money, to support yet another war of aggression. Subsequently, France was invaded, just as, by analogy, Ireland was invaded in the following century, and it is not hard to detect the same manufactured righteousness in many a war of aggression since.

In the exchanges between the king and his bishops, Shakespeare dramatizes the conflict between the requirements of a public persona and more concealed kinds of self-interest. The bishops display their ecumenical credentials and offer arguments appropriate to their station, even though we also are allowed to see their private, acquisitive concerns. For his part, the king wants to know if his royal claims and credentials are sound, so that he can invade another country with a clear conscience, based on the standards appropriate for his divinely appointed role as king. But with Henry we also feel some elements of an underlying impatience, aggravated by his personal anger at the King of France, who had insulted him, causing him now to be eager to find a pretext to get the invasion under way.

When the invasion does get going, the famous emblazoned speeches with which the brilliant Henry inspires his troops are indeed remarkable. Patriots in the audience might fairly burst with pride on hearing them, and the play as triumphant epic celebration is an impressive thing. This is the king as hero, representative of a united people fighting in a just cause. Yet, as we see, the foundations are shaky, and the more we look, the more complex Shakespeare's vision appears, as we see the uncomfortable contradictions between persona and self, public role playing and private motivation.

The play even has an Irishman in it: Captain Macmorris, who brings some of these contradictions to the surface. At one point, during a conversation with a Welsh Captain, Fluellen, Macmorris declares that he wants action: "I would have blowed up the town," he says (3.2.92), and, well, in light of recent Irish history we might recognize the flavour of that. Fluellen tries to put in a word for taking a more orderly approach, and in so doing lets slip the phrase, "Not many of your nation. . . ." The rebarbative Macmorris (the very first stage Irishman) replies: "Of my nation? What ish my nation? Ish a villain, and a basterd, and a knave, and a rascal. What ish my nation? Who talks of my nation?" (3.2.124–26).

The main idea in these slightly perplexing words is that Macmorris is angry at being identified as Irish, when the whole point about the British forces is that they unite English, Scottish, Welsh, and Irish soldiers in a grand solidarity. What do you mean by calling me Irish, Macmorris says. Would you call me a villain, or other abusive names? Well, then, don't vilify me by identifying me as an outsider to this group, this band of brothers for whom I am willing to fight and die. Here, Macmorris rejects his representative identity (as Irish) and insists that he is an individual, able to make his own allegiances, and that he should not be stereotyped.

But in Macmorris's anger, a further anxiety shows through. He realizes that in England he will appear an Irishman, and in Ireland he will appear to have sold out by joining the British army. He is touchy and sensitive about this ambivalent identity, and we might reflect on how little has changed over the centuries. But there is also a stronger point: the rhetoric of war requires an enemy — whether French or Irish — to be homogenized in order to be demonized; yet the one Irishman in the play happens to be in the king's army. As is always the case with actual people, Macmorris is not easily pigeonholed, and his identity is not simple or univocal, even though the heroes such as Henry (or Essex) need to assume otherwise to suit their own violent purposes.

In one of the play's most celebrated speeches, Henry again plays the religious card to boost the war effort. Just before the Agincourt battle, he invokes "God's will" and launches into a rousing address to his troops, taking a cue from the fact that it is St. Crispin's Day. In future years, commemorations of the saint will also be commemorations of the battle, and when the soldiers are "safe home" they will remember with pride:

And Crispin Crispian shall ne'er go by,
From this day to the ending of the world,
But we in it shall be remembered —
We few, we happy few, we band of brothers.
   (4.3.57-60)

It is a long, heady, and inspiring address, but it is interesting to notice how relentlessly it deploys the future tense. Henry begins in the present ("This day is called the feast of Crispian" [4.3.40]) but then vaults immediately into an account of commemorations that will occur much later. If religious sentiment helps to raise the spirits in hope, hope in turn lifts the gaze to a further horizon. In short, the whole thing is contrived to divert attention away from the horrifying events at hand, and the gaze is deflected so that God's work can be done in holy indifference to what it actually entails. A common soldier, Michael Williams, is allowed to reflect quietly on the night before the battle: "I am afeard there are few die well that die in a battle" (4.1.141). He then provides a daunting little sketch of amputated arms and legs and of the grief and impoverishment of widows and orphans. Henry's juggernaut, of course, remains impervious, driven by a self-righteousness that blinds him to the costs of which Williams reminds us.

And so we might see two kinds of language at work in *Henry V.* The first — exemplified by the king addressing his troops, and by the Chorus — is epic, panoramic, impersonal, idealistic, and identifies self with persona — the actual, imperfect human being with his highest ideals. The second — exemplified by Macmorris and Williams — is ordinary, conflicted, intimate, and closer to the world of the theatre than to the epic. In effect, *Henry V* can be read as an epic with a play inserted into it, and the result is that the grandly imagined heroism remains entrancing. But the dramatic, relational language of ordinary people, such as Macmorris, whose own identity is so interestingly problematic, throws into relief the shortcomings of martial heroism, as well as the cynicism of the self-aggrandizing warlords and their hirelings who deploy God and religion to aid and abet the slaughter of innocents.

Consequently, as we might have known, it is not so much Shakespeare who is worrisome as audiences and readers who swallow whole the epic dimension of *Henry V* without attending sufficiently to the play. We recall that most people in the democracies officially supporting the invasion of Iraq felt much as did Michael Williams, but, like him, were unable to prevent the war or sufficiently resist the official rhetoric that made it also seem undertaken "with right and conscience." The fact is, as Pascal says, that people never do evil so fully and so happily as when they do it for conscience's sake. We might add that, to keep their conscience clear, these same people can be counted on to drag a patriotic brand of religion in by the heels, coercing it to their purposes — whether an invasion of France,

Ireland, or somewhere else. Certainly, a righteous leader with God on his side can be counted on to ignore the diversities of ordinary life and the messy imperfections that make the boundaries between self and other permeable and flexible. By contrast, warfare requires a radical oversimplification that entails an equally radical dehumanizing — evident not least in Henry's unwavering conviction that "God fought for us."

II

Crucifying Harry
Victims, Scapegoats, and the Northern Ireland Troubles

When Shakespeare's Prince Harry became King Henry V, he also became (as he himself tells us in 2 *Henry IV*) a new man — the king who embodies and represents his people. As I have suggested in the previous chapter, that is one meaning of the term "representative identity." But there is a second meaning, which I also mentioned briefly, and which applies when a person who is identified as a member of a group is taken to represent that group, regardless of the person's own opinions and convictions. As an example, I would like to consider another Harry — Harry McCartan — a young delinquent and car thief in modern Northern Ireland. A brief outline of the Northern Ireland Troubles can set the scene within which Harry's cruel misfortune occurred.

The Troubles extended roughly from the late 1960s to the landmark Good Friday Agreement of 1998. During this period the majority unionist population (almost exclusively Protestant) sought to maintain Northern Ireland's constitutional links to Britain. An increasingly large minority of nationalists (mostly Catholic) insisted that the British should leave Ireland and that Northern Ireland become part of the Irish Republic.

The first protest marches organized on behalf of the minority population did not, however, focus on the partition question, but on civil rights. The marchers wanted to draw attention to discriminatory practices by the unionist Protestant majority against Catholics in jobs, housing, and voting. The claim was that Catholics in Northern Ireland were not being treated fairly as British citizens and that the British should see to it that the injustices were corrected. When the civil rights marches were attacked by the Northern Ireland police, the British government was forced to take action, and the army was sent to provide security. At first, the Catholic minority welcomed the soldiers. The black eye, after all, belonged to the unionists, and especially to the disgraced police. But the honeymoon was not to last.

Armed soldiers on the streets will, in all likelihood, sooner or later start shooting. Provocation, stupidity, confusion, accident, aggression, and fear are a combustible mix, plentifully supplied in Northern Ireland from many sides. All it took was a spark, and with a great number of sparks already in the air, it is hard to say which one (or how many) in fact ignited the touch paper. Accusations about who started it, who fired first, soon became irrelevant for practical purposes as the flames took hold.

With violence on the streets, now patrolled by the British army, the civil rights protest was quickly replaced by more radical demands that the British should withdraw from Northern Ireland altogether. Understandably, unionists reacted by insisting on even tighter security, calling for a beefed-up British military presence. Nationalist sentiment (inclined to be moderate) in many quarters swerved towards hard-line republicanism, calling for armed resistance. The ideals of the old Irish Republican Army (IRA), which fought for Irish independence in the early twentieth century (the result being the partition of Ireland in 1920), were revived, though not without infighting. Eventually, the Provisional I R A emerged as the most powerful of the republican paramilitary forces, and a campaign of bombing, assassination, and guerrilla warfare turned northern Ireland into a conflict zone of exceptional virulence. A convulsion of atrocities, degradations, lies, delusions, terror, cruelty, and abuses of power took its course until, by a combination of exhaustion, stalemate, and outside assistance, a workable agreement was drafted and signed in 1998 — a complex, necessary compromise.

Among many factors influencing this compromise, one in particular was not well publicized, especially outside Northern Ireland. As the conflict intensified, the I R A found itself increasingly opposed by paramilitary forces on the unionist side. Just as nationalist opinion hardened into republicanism, so unionism hardened into loyalism, and organizations such as the Ulster Defence Association (U DA) and the Ulster Volunteer Force (U V F) emerged as the mirror image of the I R A.

Initially, loyalists were slow to organize, but, among hardliners especially, their efforts gathered around a single principle — to terrorize the terrorists. The I R A, which saw itself as a freedom-fighting army, was regarded by the government as a terrorist organization, harbouring criminals. The loyalists agreed with the government about this and undertook, simply, to answer terror with terror. In so doing, they targeted ordinary Catholics in a nakedly sectarian campaign, bringing a counterterrorist terrorism literally to the doorsteps of the minority population. Some commentators think that the fearsome cruelties and increasing effectiveness of the loyalist paramilitaries were influential in causing the I R A to realize that violence could not be the answer. It is a grim fact to acknowledge, and it is not the whole story, but there is some truth in it.

After the Good Friday Agreement was signed in 1998, media focus shifted to constitutional and political events. But as a result of population shifts during the previous thirty years, housing in Northern Ireland at the time of the agreement was more segregated than ever.

Republican and loyalist estates and enclaves remained geographically separate as well as ideologically obdurate. They were governed from within, off-limits to the police, dangerous to outsiders, sustained by old animosities and by a passionately felt sense of solidarity, deeply rooted in history. Although there was a broad range of attitudes and behaviour in Northern Ireland as a whole, the political compromise — the intricately designed legal document — did not win the hearts and minds of people living in the hardline loyalist and republican enclaves. All of which brings me to my present topic, a troubling little story about two such housing estates, four years after the agreement was signed.

In 2002, Harry McCartan, aged twenty-three, was apprehended in the loyalist Seymour Hill area of Dunmurray. Harry came from the nationalist Poleglass estate, and was a notorious joyrider. That is, he stole cars and drove them dangerously and at high speed, ditching them when he was done. One report claims that he had stolen more than two hundred cars, and for his trouble he spent time in jail.

By all accounts, Harry was a reckless customer, and recklessness is made up of bravery and stupidity mixed to varying degrees. Thus, he was brave enough to steal cars from within loyalist enclaves and stupid enough to be found drunk by a group of Seymour Hill vigilantes on their own turf.

There is some suggestion that Harry was set up by people who wanted to see him dealt with, but details of this sordid little subplot remain unclear. By contrast, the main outcome of Harry's reckless behaviour is not unclear at all: he was beaten until he was unrecognizable, and was fastened to a wooden stile by six-inch nails driven through his hands. Locally and internationally, news reports described Harry's ordeal as a crucifixion, and I want to ask what is entailed by saying that.

Harry's hands nailed to a post might well evoke the judicial torture favoured in ancient Rome and made famous by the execution of Jesus. If the resemblance seems at first not especially striking, we might reflect that some thought must have gone into providing a hammer and nails, so that even the dullest among the perpetrators would have registered — especially in the context of Northern Ireland's sectarian strife — a glimmer (at least) of recognition that here, however crudely, they were enacting the ritual made famous as Christianity's chief symbol.

Still, it does not matter much what the vigilantes thought they were doing. The point is that they did in fact evoke the religious symbol in a disturbing way. Certainly, news reports seized on the point, describing Harry as a "crucified man," "crucified by vigilantes," "crucified by thugs," subjected to a "crucifixion beating" by a "crucifixion gang."

By contrast, Superintendent Gerry Murray, who investigated the incident, is reported as having "ruled out" a sectarian motive (*Telegraph,* 4 November 2002). This opinion is echoed by Chief Constable Hugh Orde, who advised caution: "It's very easy to take short snapshots of this community — the lunatic fringe. It sells newspapers. But it's not capturing the reality" (*Boston Globe,* 9 November 2002). Yet, when it comes to evading "reality," Orde and Murray seem at pains to avoid seeing the elephant in the drawing room, and in this they are followed by the imperturbable BBC (3 November 2002), which describes an "impaling attack" but scrupulously avoids any mention of religion except to quote Superintendent Murray as ruling it out. The BBC even claims that Harry's father "had no idea why his son was attacked." As we shall see, other reports attribute quite different opinions to Harry's father and to other McCartan family members. In short, the BBC (like Murray and Orde) seems largely concerned to decontaminate Harry's ordeal, cleansing it of religious infection.

Responses in Poleglass and Seymour Hill were not so fastidious. Harry's mother is reported as saying that her son "suffered like the Lord" (*Boston Globe,* 9 November 2002), and his father flatly condemned the attack as sectarian ("This is because he is a Catholic" [*Guardian,* 5 November 2002]), as did Harry's brother, who points out that the loyalists "knew that he was from Poleglass and they said 'We have got a Catholic here'" (*Ireland On-Line,* 4 November 2002).

For their part, astoundingly, some loyalists tuned right in, as ever unwilling to pass up an opportunity for bad publicity. Graffiti in and around Seymour Hill mocked at "Harry . . . also known as Jesus (Ha. Ha. Ha.)," while announcing to the world that "Joyriders will be crucified" (*Boston Globe,* 9 November 2002; *Telegraph,* 5 November 2002). Although UDA boss Jackie McDonald assured the press that the attack was not approved beforehand, he added that if UDA approval were in place, Harry "would have been nailed up in front of the estate as a warning to others" (*People,* 10 November 2002). The mixture of forced hilarity and menace in these loyalist responses, far from suppressing sectarianism, flaunts it.

The contrast between the official and local responses is all too clear: the authorities anxiously avoid the religious dimension, whereas the estate dwellers (on both sides) insist on it. We might now ask why this is so and what it might mean to say that Harry was crucified. On the one hand, he was not exactly a man of heroic virtue suffering for a high principle to which he dedicated his life, and we might hesitate to depict him too enthusiastically as Christlike. On the other hand, he was a victim, and Christ invited us to see the victimized as somehow like himself, enjoining us to treat them with compassion. Certainly, the fact that Harry was nailed to a wooden stile suggests a parallel with Jesus as victim. And insofar as Christianity is concerned with the plight of victims, it calls attention to the mechanisms of victimization and scapegoating that operate everywhere in human societies. Knowing how this is so, people who get the message (not just committed Christians) might subsequently be better able to desist from such behaviour. This is not a theological or faith-informed idea, but, rather, an aspect of Christianity that is too important to be left only to the churches and theologians. And so here I want to turn briefly to the French anthropologist and literary intellectual René Girard, who provides an account of the crucified Christ that focuses on the idea of the scapegoat victim.

Girard argues that human societies are founded on violence and are maintained by the threat of violence. This unpleasant fact is concealed as much as possible so that societies can run smoothly under a rule of law that presents itself as impartial and transcendent. Only by standing above group rivalries, feuds, and local animosities can the law quell the disruptive energies that swirl and eddy constantly through the social fabric. Yet some safe means have to be found to express and release the enmities, hatred, and rivalries which the rule of law causes people to repress, but which the law cannot fully control. Historically, religions have played a key part in helping to effect such a controlled release, and they do so through sacrifice and scapegoat rituals. That is, sacrificial victims and scapegoats become the focus of violent energies that might otherwise disrupt the social group, and these energies are allowed a cathartic release within controlled conditions. Emotional release and ritual are therefore often closely bound up together; consequently, sacrifice rituals can give rise to powerful emotions, just as spontaneous violent impulses can find expression by taking a ritual, or quasi-ritual, form.

So, yes, Harry was maimed in an act not without religious significance, in which a spontaneous catharsis of pent-up fear and hatred was released in a quasi-ritual manner evoking a crucifixion, with an uncertain degree of self-consciousness among the perpetrators. Predictably, Superintendent Murray and Chief Constable Orde attempt to regulate the local rivalries by appealing to a decontaminated, transcendent law. Yet they do so without acknowledging how, in ethnic conflict zones everywhere, imagined representations of the Other are the lifeblood of tribal hatreds and animosities ravenous for victims and fuelled always by a mixture of paranoia and resentment. In such situations, paranoia is a response to the supposition that the other group wants what you have (your job, land, assets), and resentment arises from a belief that members of the other group have access to pleasures and gratifications that you don't (a different kind of culture, sexual behaviour, attitude to work, and so on).

Unfortunately, the reckless Harry triggered both responses simultaneously. First, he was an invader from the other estate, bent on stealing property; second, he was a joyrider motivated by an anarchic pleasure principle. Harry thus assumed (or had projected upon him) a representative identity, and the subsequent transfer to a token enemy of intensely imagined fears and resentments fomented and infused by a long history of sectarianism was expressed in an act of violence clearly bearing the marks of that same sectarianism — which is to say, evoking a crucifixion. In all this, Harry himself remains eerily anonymous, his personal experience occluded by his representative status. But insofar as he was indeed crucified, the un-freedom from which Jesus's own immolation might help to liberate us (as Girard says) emerges all too clearly, yet again grotesquely triumphant. This is so because, in a parody of what it should mean, the cross on Seymour Hill was re-annexed to a group morality and to the ritual release upon a representative victim of a commonly shared hatred and fear. For their part, in ruling out a sectarian motive and the scapegoating mechanisms that accompany it, the official voices manage in the end only to avoid confronting a root cause of the vicious behavior, which they find easier to simplify than really to engage and understand.

12

Talking to the Cyclops
On Violence and Self-Destruction

In the previous chapter, I drew attention to Harry's disturbing ano-
nymity as news coverage and commentary contended about what
kind of victim he was. Here, I want to consider a little further — again
with some passing reference to Northern Ireland — the fact that in
robbing its victims of personal identity, violence is also self-destruc-
tive. As the French philosopher-theologian Simone Weil says about
the use of force: "To the same degree, though in different fashions,
those who use it and those who endure it are turned to stone." She
wrote these words in an essay on Homer's *Iliad,* and to pursue the idea
that violence dehumanizes both victims and perpetrators, I would
like to consider an episode in Homer's other great epic, *The Odyssey*.

On his return home after the Trojan war, Odysseus and his crew
stop at an island near a land inhabited by one-eyed giants called
Cyclopes. These creatures live in isolation from one another and have

little knowledge of human community, relationship, or hospitality. Odysseus visits the cave of one of them, Polyphemos, but when Odysseus makes an introductory speech, Polyphemos does not answer. Instead, he picks up two of Odysseus's twelve companions by the heels and smashes their brains out on the floor, "like killing puppies." He then devours the dead men and rolls a giant boulder across the mouth of the cave to prevent the others from escaping. Later, he devours two more men, and gets drunk on the wine Odysseus had brought as a gift.

As the Cyclops lies deeply asleep, Odysseus and his remaining crew prepare a wooden stake, hardening the sharpened point in the fire, and then ramming it into the Cyclops's eye. The blinded Polyphemos rolls back the boulder to seek help, and by and by Odysseus and his men escape. As he sets sail, Odysseus tauntingly reveals his name (he had concealed it earlier) and mocks at his distressed and raging enemy. But the elated Odysseus has not fully considered that the Cyclops's father is Poseidon, god of the seas on which Odysseus must sail. The vengeful Poseidon — able now to identify his son's enemy by name — ensures that Odysseus's journey is disastrous, filled with misfortune, wreckage, and death.

Clearly, there is no talking to Polyphemos, bent on violence: no appeal could be made that would not merely confirm the terrifying gap between language and the sudden, shocking deaths of the men. Yet, equally clearly, Polyphemos does not imagine the consequences of his actions for himself. He is blinded physically, not least because he is already blind to the fact that violence begets violence unpredictably.

For his part, the altogether-too-smart Odysseus, whose desperate resourcefulness has saved the day, cannot contain himself, and his triumphalist bragging ends up eventually costing the lives of his entire crew at the hands of Poseidon. Like the primitive weapon he used in the cave, Odysseus's mockery is crude, turning the Cyclops into an object of contempt, just as the crewmen were nothing more than puppies to the Cyclops. In short, violence on both sides — whether we condone it or not — depersonalizes, and when it occurs, language either fails or is debased. Moreover, in response to the invasion of archaic terror and disorientation that violence brings with it, Polyphemos and Odysseus, not surprisingly, appeal to the gods — to Poseidon (for vengeance) and Athene (for deliverance).

Homer's ancient story is not just an engaging fiction; it is exigent, telling us that we cannot talk to the Cyclops who has decided on violence, and if we do it won't matter. This is because speech involves relationship, requiring mutual understanding, but violence depersonalizes and silences its victims. Today, paramilitaries wear masks and their victims are blindfolded or otherwise "disappeared." In Northern Ireland, the Shankill Butcher, Lenny Murphy, finished off one of his victims with a spade, smashing in his face after having first removed his teeth with pliers. The killers of ex-IRA member Eamon Collins mutilated him and seem to have run a car over his head to finish the job. The effect in both cases was to render the victim faceless and voiceless — not a person — by an extreme objectification, the ferocity of which betrays how desperate is the anxiety to conceal or obliterate the fact that your victim is your fellow creature, a person like yourself.

In turn, such anxiety is often so powerful that God needs to be called upon to allay it. Thus, a pamphlet entitled *Is There Room in Heaven for Billy Wright?* was issued by supporters of the Loyalist Volunteer Force (LVF) founder after his death. Of course the authors assure us that there is room in heaven for Billy and that the faithful should follow his Christian example. Presumably, in his celestial quarters Billy at this moment is graciously enjoying the company of his erstwhile mortal enemy, Bobby Sands, the Irish Republican Army (IRA) hunger striker whose Christlikeness was proclaimed with equal conviction by his backers. God, it seems, takes care of Billy and Bobby together, and they are condemned now to love one another for eternity. Meanwhile, the tribal factions on earth will, according to taste, go on consigning each of them to eternal perdition — that further grotesque idea produced out of the apparently bottomless human capacity for rage, vindictiveness, and cruelty.

Mutual accusation along such lines becomes rapidly as futile as the muddled and contemptible actions that have given rise to it and to the further primitive superstitions brought to bear by way of obfuscation and excuse. Meanwhile, the violence goes on replicating itself with the same predictable unpredictability. Yet, as it happens, the Greek thinkers who tried to make sense out of the issues raised by Homer's epics ended up also giving to Christianity a conceptual apparatus that has helped to explain the Bible — that compendium of books not without its own collusions in foisting human psychopathic behaviour upon God. Still, at best, the confluence of the Hellenic and Biblical traditions can also offer an antidote to their own disturbing witness to the worst that humans do.

Thus, if God is love, as John assures us (1 John 4:16), and if we think about this claim with respect for the conceptual consistency that philosophy prescribes, then it follows that God does not hate and is not vengeful. You cannot be love and express hate. Therefore God does not have enemies (this is true whether God exists or not), and even though you and I might make God (or the good) our enemy, it is folly to claim that God hates us back, or hates our enemies as we do (whether Billy or Bobby). In this view, the phenomenon wrongly described as God's wrath can be nothing other than our own anger and hatred experienced in the light of what love and the good really are — in short, the hot stake of our own hatred being driven back into our own eye.

When alienation and anger are displaced onto God it is indeed a good deal easier for people to get on with destroying their enemies, calling them God's enemies, but this self-deception requires such people to ignore a further basic point on which Christian theology insists, namely that God is a community of persons — three of whom constitute the Trinity. Whatever else God might or might not be — empty category or omnipotent creator — matters nothing in comparison to the only certain thing, which is that we find our good in and through persons in relationship, persons in community. To work with that principle in mind, aiming to shape a society in which the personal is political, is, in the end, the only way to mitigate the petrifying alienations that produced Polyphemos in the first place. The chances then at least are better of enabling the growth and development of individuals with whom we might talk, person to person. If the intention is good, Matthew tells us, then our whole body is filled with light because we see with a single eye (6:22). The unpredictable then is less likely to take us by surprise, even though it is prudent to remember that, short of the good society and without sufficient good fortune, the Cyclopes spawned in the wastelands of alienation and in the ghettoes of heartless privilege will still have us for dinner, without a word.

13

Doing Nothing About It
Taoism, Selflessness, and Non-Action

So far, I have considered some aspects of how the self is flexible, frag-mented, tentatively emergent, and how easily we depersonalize others by denying them a sense of selfhood such as we ourselves experience. But there is another, more positive kind of selflessness that is also worth considering, and which is connected to the kind of unself-conscious, spontaneous action that is a result of patiently acquired skill. The best kinds of human performance demonstrate this. For instance, the skilled musician is immersed in the music, and the good of the performance transcends egotism. The talented running back dodges and feints, immersed in the action and, in a sense, losing himself in the skill he demonstrates. But at the moment when self-consciousness enters in, the performance is stalled, or contaminated by showing off — an unpleasant self-aggrandizing that diminishes the achievement and the achiever.

I want now to think a little further about the kind of selflessness that is not so much a suppression of the self as a transcendence of it. To do so, I would like to consider three classical Taoist books that are especially sensitive to the paradoxes of individual selfhood in relation to the universal laws that remain the same for all. In the idea of *wu wei,* or actionless action, which these books also explore, this paradox engages with the self-transcending type of skilled performance that I have been describing.

Taoism is an ancient wisdom tradition indigenous to China. Its beginnings are in prehistoric shamanism, but over the centuries it developed as a complex body of philosophical speculation, meditative practice, and religious observance. The famous opening line of the most famous Taoist classical text, the *Tao Te Ching,* warns us against trying to define the topic too closely: "The Tao that can be told is not the eternal Tao." There is a wordplay here, because Tao means "way" or "path," but also "to speak." So you can't speak about the way without your words tripping over themselves, falling into themselves, as it were. But the wordplay also confirms the main sense of the translation: however you describe it, the Tao won't be what you say it is.

Still, there is nothing too remarkable in this assurance that words do not express the mystery of existence in which we find ourselves caught up. Theologians and philosophers in many traditions make similar observations, and the idea is also plain enough common sense. "There are more things in heaven and earth, Horatio, / Than are dreamt of in your philosophy" (1.5.166–67), Hamlet says to his scholarly friend. But what kind of philosopher would Horatio be if he did not know this? Of course there is more to heaven and earth than language, and we do not need a philosopher like Horatio (or a clever-pants like Hamlet) to tell us this.

And yet, paradoxically, the *Tao Te Ching* also assures us that there is indeed a way, or path — Tao — as each of us needs to discover. Although we cannot properly describe the Tao, it seems that we can experience it, and even learn to follow it.

The difficulty of dealing with the Tao as a concept is matched by the historical complexity of Taoism over the centuries. Although the classical texts of the Warring States period (475–221 BCE) discuss the way and how to follow it, their authors would not have thought of themselves as Taoists — that is, as members of a school or movement. Nonetheless, many schools and movements did arise, teaching meditation, alchemy, and the pursuit of immortality. When Buddhism reached China at the start of the Common Era, it merged readily with these native currents of thought and practice. Various combinations of Taoism, Buddhism, and Confucianism then rapidly produced an overgrowth of practices, ideas, and systems mingling ancient folk beliefs with philosophical reflection, medical lore, religious observance, cult practice, and esoteric techniques for internal transformation.

Consequently, there is no standard approach to Taoism; instead, we each have to find a particular path into the discussion, just as we each have to encounter the Tao in a particular way in our own lives. With this in mind, I confine myself here to three famous classical texts, ascribed to Lao Tzu, Chuang Tzu, and Lieh Tzu. Lao Tzu wrote the *Tao Te Ching;* the other two wrote books that bear their names — the *Book of Chuang Tzu,* or simply the *Chuang Tzu,* and the *Lieh Tzu.* Also, I want to focus on the idea of *wu wei,* which is central to all three texts and is usually translated as "non-action" or "actionless action" but which also carries the sense of acting spontaneously.

It can be a seductive notion, that non-action achieves more than action; that letting-it-be is more advantageous than always being-at-it; that going with the flow is the best way. The (apparent) quietism of these sorts of ideas was, for instance, especially attractive to the counterculture of the 1960s, which did much to popularize Taoism in the West. But it is worth noticing also that a good many of the 1960s dropouts were happy to climb back on board as the reviled corporations marketed their music, turning rebellion into nostalgia. Reaganomics and Thatcherism emerged in the ascendant, unperturbed by the flowers in the gun barrels, and revolution-lite did not, in the end, put much hurt on the military-industrial complex.

Yet, in a larger and more interesting sense, the 1960s interest in Eastern religions and religious philosophies can be seen also as an offshoot of that important earlier movement of protest and affirmation that we know as Romanticism. The heartbeat of the Romantic movement was the idea that nature should be trusted. A millennium and a half of Christian theology had promoted the contrary idea that, despite the original goodness of God's creation, nature is fallen. As the redoubtable Augustine says, each of us is a *massa damnata,* a "damned lump," and only God's grace can restore us. Augustine's doctrine of original sin underlies the general Christian, specifically Puritan, subjection of the passions, but it also shaped the preconceptions and aspirations of early modern science, which sought to subject a hostile nature in the interests of improving the human lot.

By proclaiming the innocence of childhood and nature's nurturing beneficence, the Romantics of the early nineteenth century sought to let go of both Puritan self-hatred and the Faustian compulsion to dominate and control the natural world. The contest between a Romantic affirmation of nature and the scientific conquest of it continues to the present, even though religion no longer governs the debate from the centre. Modern secularism — itself an offshoot of the great prestige of modern science — has driven a wedge between religion and science, religion and politics. Today, original sin, hell, and damnation no longer pass muster as the dominant ideology, and one appeal of Eastern religions in the second half of the twentieth century has been to provide an alternative to these tired doctrines, but in a way that also addresses the Romantic critique of scientific instrumentalism. Taoism is a case in point. It does not posit a creator God and has no theory of original sin. Rather, we are asked to trust nature and to discover the Tao for ourselves by harmonizing with the great sustaining rhythms of the natural world. The values here are broadly Romantic — critical of conventional morality and vigorously individualistic.

Seen in this light, Taoism, for Westerners, enters into an already complex cultural debate. The 1960s counterculture preferred to opt out of the debate altogether and to start afresh, seeing in Eastern religions the possibility of a new beginning. But, ironically, the desire to opt out presupposes a prior immersion, and attempting to turn away and let things be can be rapidly enervating rather than liberating.

Still, our three Taoist authors are clear in recommending the advantages of non-action. "The sage goes about doing nothing" (4), says Lao Tzu; "Don't struggle, go with the flow," says Chuang Tzu (56); "The best way to get things done is not to do them," says Lieh Tzu. What, then, does Taoism teach that is different from the unwitting apostles of enervation who advise us just to let go and drop out?

First, it is worth noticing that Lao Tzu, Chuang Tzu, and Lieh Tzu are very different, and part of the enjoyment of reading them is to discover how this is so. Lao Tzu is elusive, oracular, teasing us to follow his meaning. Chuang Tzu is rambunctious, full of crazy humour and extravagant allegory, deliberately provoking us. Lieh Tzu is companionable, an engaging storyteller who affirms our ordinary common sense and who understands our fallibilities. Still, despite these differences, all three have in common a single, governing insight which they share with other breakthrough thinkers of the so-called Axial Age, such as Isaiah, Socrates, Plato, Gautama Buddha, and Jesus. This insight resides in the discovery of the self as an autonomous moral agent, and requires that we must step outside the bonds and prescriptions of family, caste, ritual observance, custom, and group identity in order to make independent moral choices. The mystery of origins, the one reality beyond language and beyond concepts, the transcendent which is also immanent, is ours to seek and to experience individually. By comparison with the integrity of that interior observance, external factors such as cult practice, social or family obligation, and the like are held to be insignificant. The classical Taoist texts deliver this message from within their own cultural circumstances, and each author's distinctive voice exemplifies the main point — the transcendent, the Tao, is to be experienced individually. I want to suggest that, read in such a context, the idea of *wu wei* is not just about letting go; it is about the process by which we find our way as autonomous selves in a world where the only constant is impermanence.

Lao Tzu is quite straightforward about the advantages of doing nothing: "If nothing is done, then all will be well" (5); "Are you able to do nothing?" (12); "Tao abides in non-action" (39). Yet, paradoxically, he also tells us that a "good man" who does nothing "leaves nothing undone" (40) — a point he then repeats (50). The paradoxical interrelationship here between not-doing and doing lies at the heart of Lao Tzu's view of effective human agency, which he sees as a combination, as it were, of soft and hard. Thus, we will "know the value of non-action" if we understand how "the softest thing in the universe / Overcomes the hardest thing in the universe" (45). In this, the Tao is like water, "soft and yielding," and yet "for attacking the solid and strong, nothing is better" (80). Water can wear away rocks; yet it "does not strive" but "flows in places men reject and so is like the Tao" (10).

Non-action, then, does not mean that nothing gets done. After all, the *Tao Te Ching* offers advice to political leaders, and a good ruler must "achieve results" (32). Lao Tzu asks us to consider, simply, that yielding, which is non-action, can be effective: "A tree that is unbending is easily broken" (78). That is, mere force — an excess of male *yang* energy — is vulnerable because it is rigid and needs tempering by the soft and flexible, the female *yin*. Thus, "The hard and strong will fall. / The soft and weak will overcome" (78).

The *Tao Te Ching* tells us this in various ways, for instance by explaining the usefulness of the hub (an empty space) to the wheel (13), and having us understand that the emptiness of a hollow vessel makes the vessel useful (13). By analogy, darkness and silence are gates to the great mystery of the Tao, as is the hollow of the valley, for "The valley spirit never dies; / It is the woman, primal mother" (87). "Can you play the role of woman?" Lao Tzu asks — which is to say, can you be "open to all things, / Are you able to do nothing?" (12).

> Know the strength of man
> But keep a woman's care!
> Be the stream of the universe! (30)

Strength, here, is not dismissed. But strength without flexibility, nurture, reciprocity, is ineffective. "Stream of the universe" returns us to the water motif and to the power of what is apparently weak. As we read on, we discover that this stream is also the great double movement of the Tao which expresses itself in all things and is the source to which all things return. And so we are folded into the soft embrace of Lao Tzu's seductively gentle acquiescence in the "natural way" (32), assured that "the world is ruled by letting things take their course" (50). But Lao Tzu is also steely, and his writing has the same combination of flexibility and strength as his thinking advocates. "Know the white, / But keep the black" (30), he tells us, for neither *yang* nor *yin* alone will do. Whether we rule a country or ourselves according to what the *Tao Te Ching* tells us, we need to learn the art of doing nothing but leaving nothing undone. Lao Tzu does not tell us much in detail about how to acquire this art. Chuang Tzu fills out the picture.

The *Chuang Tzu* mentions Lao Tzu by name but has no direct quotation from the *Tao Te Ching*. It seems likely that both authors drew on a common stock of oral teachings, but less likely that Chuang Tzu had read Lao Tzu's book. The textual questions here are complex and dates are indefinite. The shadowy figure of Lao Tzu (who might not have existed as an actual person) is associated with a set of texts thought to date, roughly, from the sixth to the fifth century BCE. Chuang Tzu lived some two hundred years later (as did Lieh Tzu), and in Chuang Tzu's eyes, Lao Tzu is a revered teacher.

Still, there is no mistaking the special character of these two books. Chuang Tzu is wild and eclectic — by turns satirical, allegorical, comic, aphoristic, and filled with anecdotes confirming a zany nonconformism. Like Lao Tzu, he reminds us of the insufficiency of words ("Who knows the argument that needs no words, and the Tao that cannot be named?" [16]). But then he also notices that, well, he has been using words to say that words are unimportant (15). By and by we learn that he deliberately resorts to paradox, "strange and mysterious expressions, wild and extraordinary phrases, and terms which had no precise meaning" (304). His teachings remain "difficult and subtle" (304) because they are so self-consciously — at times, even, perversely — indirect, and this is what we find also when he deals with *wu wei*.

In approaching the topic, Chuang Tzu invokes the old master: "Lao Tzu said, 'Know the masculine but hold to the feminine, become the valley of the whole world.'" Whoever does this lives "by actionless action" and is "free to bend and twist" because "that which is strong will break" (303). As in the *Tao Te Ching*, the female, which is also the valley, represents flexibility, which is necessary for true strength, and finding a balance between strength and yielding is, again, the key to "actionless action." Still, we find all this also in Lao Tzu, and for the extra dimension that Chuang Tzu provides, we need to look at his understanding of how actionless action might be acquired. Again, we are not instructed by precept but by an indirection that is analogous to the indirect means by which we are also to acquire the art of non-action.

For instance, Lord Wen Hui admires the extraordinary skill displayed by his cook, who is butchering an ox, and asks for an explanation. The cook begins by saying that he loves the Tao, and then explains how his skill developed over many years, so that now he practises without attending to his physical movements, seeing immediately "the natural lines" (23) through which his knife glides effortlessly. Without deliberation, he knows the spaces between the joints, into which the thin blade passes without resistance. In full possession of his skill, the butcher explains how he can "ignore my sense and follow my spirit" (23). His skill is deployed unselfconsciously, and this also is what we are to know when we act in tune with the Tao.

The same point is made in a story about the Grand Marshal's swordsmith, who is eighty years old and has been making swords since he was twenty. The Grand Marshal admires the swordsmith's skill and asks, "Do you have the Tao?" The swordsmith replies, "I do have the Tao," and goes on to explain that during his long career he has been entirely and exclusively devoted to making swords: "I pay no heed to anything else," and "by being so constant I am now able to do it without thinking. Time brings one to such art" (196). Here again, skill that is developed through long practice becomes so internalized that the practitioner does not think about how it operates. In medieval Europe, craftsmen were said to have a "mystery," meaning the uncanny expertise that is the result of a long apprenticeship. Chuang Tzu would have understood this exactly, and it is what he means also by living according to the Tao, exercising the mystery of "actionless action."

The third classic text is the book of Lieh Tzu, in which, again, we quickly recognize some familiar motifs. As with Lao Tzu and Chuang Tzu, the "Mysterious Female" or "Valley Spirit" reminds us that we do not control our coming into this world, and we need to yield to the unrepresentable power of the "not-born," the "Gate of the Mysterious Female" where "all things are created" (27). As in Lao Tzu, "strength should always be complemented by softness. If you resist too much, you will break" (78). Finding a balance between the hard and soft remains for Lieh Tzu the key to enlightenment, which, in turn, is the natural way (135). All of which brings us once more to non-action, the art of letting go, relinquishing control to bring about the most effective result: "By knowing and doing nothing, you can know and do all" (31). This art of "doing nothing" is not the same as inertia; rather, it calls for disciplined attention and practice.

Chuang Tzu's butcher and swordsmith have their counterparts in Lieh Tzu's fisherman (140) and charioteer (154), who also acquire their skill patiently, so that it becomes internalized and they act unselfconsciously. Thus, the apprentice charioteer Tsao-fu learns to jump on a set of upright posts so that he can acquire agility and balance. Eventually, when this skill is transferred to the control of horses, the driver's body will be so sensitive to shifts in balance that the horses are controlled as if "by intention alone." "Agility of body and stillness of mind are required for attention to be communicated naturally" (155); that is, through practice, the mind seems not to control the body, and harmony is achieved as if without effort. As Lieh Tzu says, "Knowing how to act and not using effort to do it, is the mark of a sage" (128).

Yet Lieh Tzu is also his own man, and the impress of an individual sensibility makes his book as distinctive as are the other two. For instance, he makes a special point of reminding us that people are not perfect, and he draws attention, humourously, to his own flaws. He fails an archery test and breaks into a cold sweat (58). Elsewhere, he realizes his learning is shallow and he lacks understanding (70). In short, he is more recognizably an ordinary person than are Lao Tzu and Chuang Tzu. He insists that "someone who is enlightened does not appear perfect" (74), and "Enlightenment is a very normal experience, attainable by everyone. Therefore, there is nothing mysterious or secretive about it" (117). We are told at the start that Lieh Tzu was "unassuming" (25) and never made a name for himself. His core message is that reputation, power, titles, and the like are not worth the sacrifice of our health or peace of mind. For Lieh Tzu, the skill required for *wu wei* comes by trial and error, and in the most ordinary circumstances. People blunder despite their good intentions, and human fallibility and imperfection are also part of the process, part of what the way entails.

To summarize: These three books agree that the unnameable Tao is the same for all because it is the source and origin of all, and yet it is different for each because we travel our own way individually. "Death," Lieh Tzu says, is "a kind of homecoming," and "a living person is a traveling person" (40). Like each of us, the world's great cultures also travel their own way, and the Taoist classics are rewarding and engaging for Western readers partly because of their cultural differences as they provide a refreshing, provocative account of how the Tao moves through all things, how we should trust nature and ourselves as part of nature. These books engage also with matters of perennial concern — the hunger for power, the illusions of fame, the mystery of existence, the quest for virtue, the puzzle of death, the challenges of the great movement of transformation as things emerge into a splendour of individual forms and are then drawn back to the source by a great movement of return.

Yet Taoism can be seductively easy to misread, and this is certainly so in the case of the intriguing notion of "non-action." As we see, *wu wei* does not mean giving up and dropping out; rather, it describes the effortlessness of consummate skill, the result of dedicated practice entailing an exact harmony of opposites — the hard and soft, *yang* and *yin*, strength and flexibility. Just so, reading Taoism in the context of the core debate between science and Romanticism calls for dialogue, an encounter between different traditions in which the identity of neither is relinquished even as the Spirit, the Tao, declares itself in what goes between the opposites, gathering them into its ineffable energy.

From my own perspective within such a dialogue across the traditions in question, I believe Lao Tzu when he says that "heaven and earth are impartial" (7); Chuang Tzu when he says that "the Tao has neither beginning nor end, but all living things have both death and birth, so you cannot be sure of them" (142); Lieh Tzu when he says, "All things come and go without the need of a creator or a mover" (172). These opinions are appealing because they hold in counterpoint the imponderable mystery of the universe and the imperfect understanding of each individual person who negotiates the way that is his or hers alone. This being the case, there is some comfort in the open-endedness both of ourselves and of our continuing, unfinished dialogue with others who are likewise finding their way by means of the careful practice that makes a person's best skills unselfconscious and, in the good sense, selfless.

14

Cliff Jumpers and Delta Dwellers
On Religious Language and Commitment

I have been suggesting that such things as personal identity, self-worth, and responsibility depend on commitments to ideals through which, in turn, we discover our imperfections. In the previous chapters of this section I have dealt with various aspects of this set of issues: how we might assess responsibility, given that the self can change over time; how dominant ideas about society and about the self mirror each other; how identifying with the persona can cause dangerous ego-inflation; how representative identity leads to scapegoating; how violence is destructive of one's self as well as of others; how skilled performance is self-transcending.

In each of these cases, an ideal value frames a commitment which is then tested against the refractory world of actual experience. A great deal depends on whether or not such commitments end up being life-affirming rather than merely oppressive — annexed, that is, to a deadening conservatism behind which it can be inviting to huddle for safety against the ungovernable horror and beauty of what lies beyond. I would like now briefly to say something more about these two faces of commitment — the life-affirming and the oppressive.

Interestingly, religious language — which is especially geared to encourage commitment — has always relied heavily on non-literal meanings; that is, in religion, words often are used in ways that direct our attention to something other than what the words are usually taken to signify. This has been (and is) a source of confusion not only about language but also about the commitments religion requires; moreover, the results of this confusion have frequently been harmful.

For instance, in the Christian doctrine of the Trinity, the Father, Son, and Holy Spirit are described as Three Persons in One Nature. Theologians agree that reason alone could not arrive at such a definition; rather, the Trinity is revealed by God's grace through holy scripture, from which, in turn, the theological formulation is deduced. It took hundreds of years to get the formulation right, in the course of which heresies arose and were condemned (Arian, Nestorian, Eutychian, Sabellian, among others). Throughout this immense debate, scrupulous consideration was given to Greek and Latin words for what we call in English "nature," "person," "relation," and to what might be meant by "Father," "Son," and "Holy Spirit." The language in which such matters were discussed is for the most part abstract, but the debate is also at times weirdly passionate, as we see, for instance, in the case of Maximus Confessor, a seventh-century Greek Church Father.

Maximus argued that because Christ, Second Person of the Trinity, had a divine and a human nature, he must have a divine and a human will. When Maximus refused to change his mind about this unacceptable theory, the authorities had his right hand amputated and his tongue cut out (these body parts, presumably, representing writing and speech). He died soon after.

The theological definition must have meant a lot to Maximus — certainly, a lot more than it means to most of us today. For us, such controversy will likely seem formulaic and abstract, definitely not worth the passionate investment Maximus made in it. Yet the fact is that today we easily replace one set of words-to-die-for with others — Catholic, Protestant, Sunni, Shia, Jew, Great Satan, Anti-Christ, to name a few — not to mention the names of numerous ethnic groups in conflict zones across the globe, for whom religion is a key marker of identity. And so we might pause to wonder what degree of credibility, if any, we can accord to language expressing religious commitment, and why such language can be compelling to believers and in some instances sympathetically received also by unbelievers (though in other instances emphatically not).

To begin, let us return to the idea that the doctrine of the Trinity could not be discovered by reason alone. Theologians who make this point will also hasten to assure us that saying a thing is non-rational is not the same as saying that it is irrational. For instance, you might choose to marry, drawn by another person's allure beyond the scope of your reason to describe. Insofar as your choice (thankfully, in this case) is not reducible to reason alone, it is non-rational. But if you choose to marry because you are convinced that the other person is a robot from Mars come to show you the secrets of time travel, then you are being irrational. The main point here is that reason can be filled out and completed by disclosures beyond the reach of reason itself; by contrast, reason is merely defeated and diminished by irrationality.

It is (one hopes) clear today that what was done to Maximus shows reason defeated and diminished, and it is difficult to understand how an abstract debate about the meaning of persons could have such a horrifying consequence. What were they thinking, those tormentors in the name of Christ? The case that a conscientious Christian might make to explain the abstract debate (as distinct from its consequences) might begin by asking us to recall that an old word for "creed" is *symbolon* (symbol), indicating that there is something non-literal or symbolic about the theological language that creeds deploy. So, for instance, the word "person" as applied to God

135

is intended to appear reasonable to us but also to point to something beyond reason. It is reasonable because we like to think God cares for us, is in dialogue with us, and allows our freedom. Such things can be well described as "personal," even though God is not another person just like us. After all, God created us (and everything else), and as creatures we are less than God, the all-encompassing mystery. Consequently, the value we place on persons, relationship, dialogue, and freedom is a value we also attribute to God even though God is infinitely more. Also, because theological language makes claims about the Absolute (which we can never understand), such claims are asserted at last by way of conviction — a hunch about the ultimate goodness of the universe, going beyond reason but without being irrational.

All of which brings me now to the (non-literal) Cliff Jumpers of my title. Imagine that you are standing alone on a thirty-foot cliff, looking down at the sea. You notice the elegant curve of a deep-running current, and a stiff breeze agitates the water into a mesh of small, blustery waves. Then an inflated rubber ring comes into view, being drawn slowly out to sea. You think you might like to have this rubber ring, but soon decide that, even though you swim well, you aren't going to risk the jump, the choppy sea, and the current. That is a reasonable decision.

Now imagine yourself again in the same situation, except that this time there is a child in the rubber ring, kept afloat but nonetheless being swept away. In this situation you might decide to jump. After all, you are a good swimmer, it's only thirty feet into deep water, you think you have a chance, and your decision is on the side of life — in rescuing the child, you will prevent a life from being swallowed up by chaos. But you might be wrong, and you and the child might drown. Reason alone can't decide the issue, but it is not irrational to jump.

The main difference between these two situations is that we attach a greater value to the child than to the rubber ring, and the value being greater makes the risk more worthwhile. This example can, now, represent for our conscientious believer what, at best, religious language attempts to do. Basically, it takes a chance that our central, life-affirming experiences are tokens of reality as a whole, and, in so doing, it gambles on rescuing life from chaos. Yet such commitment remains a gamble, a leap of faith best represented symbolically and best appreciated by considering the spirit in which it is undertaken, affirming the value of life. Should you drown trying to rescue the child, I would admire and respect you for the leap you took. As Karen Armstrong correctly says in *The Spiral Staircase* (New York: Alfred A. Knopf, 2004), there "may be nothing out there," but the main task of religion is nonetheless to "mend our broken world," and if religion can't attend to this task, then it is "worthless" (304). That is, religious commitment needs to be on the side of life as we know it here and now.

But the Cliff Jumpers are only one part of our story, and religions also have their (again non-literal) Delta Dwellers. As their name suggests, Delta Dwellers live on flat land, in estuaries where the great river divides and subdivides into a network of streams in its final push to the sea. These streams shape the delta into islands, and each island is inhabited by a group of people who claim exclusive rights to their own piece of land. To confirm these rights, each group maintains as a matter of religious conviction that the streams defining and irrigating its territory are, in fact, the main river, whereas the other streams are offshoots, subsidiary outflows from the source. Territorialism and exclusivism flourish on the fertile soil of such conviction, and the history of religions is mainly a history about Delta Dwellers — that is, about the maintenance of orthodoxy, definition of boundaries, exclusion of non-believing outsiders, and curtailment of dissenting enquiry. Moreover, in making their case, Delta Dwellers readily adopt, mimic, or misuse the Cliff Jumpers' language and aspirations. In so doing, they often don't much bother to notice the elisions and contradictions between their declared idealism and actual practice.

Examples are not hard to find, and polemicists against religion have no difficulty in having a field day. For instance, Richard

Dawkins asks us to consider Gary Potter, President of Catholics for Christian Political Action, who promises that when a Christian majority takes over the United States, "pluralism will be seen as immoral and evil and the state will not permit anybody the right to practice evil." In much the same spirit, US evangelist Pat Robertson advises his followers that homosexuals "want to come into churches and disrupt church services and throw blood all around and try to give people AIDS and spit in the face of ministers" (*The God Delusion* [Boston: Houghton Mifflin, 2006], 290). Christopher Hitchens points out that the Dalai Lama says it is acceptable to visit a prostitute, but someone else has to pay her. Along the same lines, some Shia Muslims "offer 'temporary marriage,' selling men permission to take a wife for an hour or two with the usual vows and then divorce her when they are done" (*God Is Not Great* [Toronto: McClelland and Stewart, 2007], 212). Michel Onfray cites Pope John Paul II as arguing that the atom bomb opened the road to peace, and Father George Zabelka blessed the crew of the *Enola Gay* before they took off to drop the bomb on Hiroshima on 6 August 1945 (*In Defense of Atheism* [Toronto: Viking, 2007], 192). Admittedly, no one should expect a completely desanitized engagement between religion and the complex affairs of the world. But the combination of punitive resentment, proscription, and hypocritical deception evident even in this meagre sample of what has been claimed by true believers is dismaying, to say the least.

Certainly, the religions also provide examples of courage and compassion, of remarkable people taking a generous risk for life. But it does not matter if the generous risk is taken in the name of a religious creed or not. A main achievement of secularism has been to reverse the ages-old conviction that religion is the arbiter of morals. No, we are now able to say, morality is the criterion without which religion itself is beside the point. And so, whether they are professedly religious or not, our Cliff Jumpers do a good thing in acting to preserve life from chaos and to value individual persons here and now. Delta Dwellers can be counted on to resist this conclusion, and we can be sure that, if they could, they would have our right hand off and our tongue out for insisting on the point in the first place.

Life-affirming or not? What are the consequences of commitment in the shaping of the selves that we take ourselves to be? And to what extent are we free to choose our commitments in the first place? To address these issues more fully, let us now move to the final section, on freedom.

PART III *Freedom*

15

Dr. Johnson, Freedom, and the Book of Psalms

The exercise of freedom is central to the sense we have of ourselves as moral agents. But what if our autonomy is an illusion, a concealment of the fact that we aren't aware of the intricate chains of cause and effect determining our actions? How do we know which choices are free, and to what extent are we driven by forces beyond our understanding? As I mentioned in the Introduction, the Bible is less concerned with the philosophical aspects of freedom than with human responsibility before God and with the burden of guilt and the aspirations to deliverance that are a consequence of our dangerous but God-given ability to choose. I would like now to consider how the Bible — specifically, the Book of Psalms — imparts this vision of human moral agency. But to frame the discussion I will begin by considering briefly the philosophical puzzle, to which I will then return in conclusion.

When Samuel Johnson's biographer, James Boswell, goaded the great man to comment on God's foreknowledge in relation to human free will, he found himself quickly and tidily dispatched. "All theory is against the freedom of the will; all experience for it," Johnson replied, and then: "Sir, we *know* our will is free, and *there's* an end on it" (*Life of Samuel Johnson* [New York: Everyman's Library, 1906], 833 and 366).

Johnson makes his case largely by refusing to debate the question, and he smartly short-circuits further argument by allowing that "theory" favours the determinist position. Presumably, this is so because theoretical explanations focus on cause and effect, but freedom is, precisely, that which is uncaused, and consequently it eludes explanation. Rather, we experience freedom directly in our day-to-day lives as a kind of bodily-rooted knowledge. As Johnson says, "You are surer that you can lift up your finger or not as you please, than you are of any conclusion from a deduction of reasoning."

Johnson's main point is that for practical purposes we need to choose rather than ponder too closely how an action is the product of a chain of causes, or what part it might play in God's plan. Although we should try to make informed decisions, thinking "too precisely on th' event" (as Hamlet says) soon immobilizes us. The philosopher Jean-Paul Sartre cites the example of a man unable to choose an item from a menu because he gets so overwhelmed by the awareness of being free to do so. Johnson would remind the man that he needs to get on with his lunch.

Yet most of us will have experienced a moment like Sartre's man with the menu, hesitating to make a simple choice because of the sheer strangeness of being able to choose at all. Imagining the imponderable consequences and incalculable circumstances that weigh upon the moment from the obscurities of a largely unknowable future and a largely irrecoverable past might understandably pitch a person into confusion. Nor is it the case that too much thinking simply prevents action; it can also cause people to choose downright badly. Anyone who has worked on large committees will know how too many voices striving to make a contribution can result in a committee doing exactly other than the obviously right thing. Smaller groups often do better because they are better able to feel themselves part of a single entity, capable of making a focused decision, yet without losing the advantage of differing points of view. And so it seems that too much or too little reasoning can equally prevent us from choosing well. The trick is to get the balance right.

So far, I have not distinguished between the determinist who sees choice as the product of material causes and effects, and the religious believer — such as Johnson — who allows that God already knows everything that will happen, including what choices we will make. Both agree that there is, as it were, an overarching order to which we have real but limited access. Nonetheless, within this containing design, believers and non-believers for the most part go on treating themselves and others as having intentions, values, responsibilities, and some degree of autonomy. Believers often go to great lengths to show that God's foreknowledge is compatible with human free will, and most non-believing materialists consider that morality entails some degree of personal autonomy. Again, balance is the key to maintaining a (relatively) healthy-minded disposition on the question.

Still, a believer might tip this balance by thinking too scrupulously about what God knows, and as a result might embrace predestinationism — the conviction that he or she is already damned or saved and can do nothing about it because God has already decided. Likewise, the overly rational unbeliever might sink into a nihilistic hopelessness under the burden of a meaningless universe unfolding through a blind, impersonal mechanism. In both cases, the idea of a seamless, overarching order is oppressive if it is thought about too closely, and on such matters, Dr. Johnson in his personal life was himself inclined to be neurotic rather than healthy-minded. In his bluff response to Boswell we might feel some degree of anxious avoidance as he insists on the paradox, partly to convince himself (rather than just Boswell) not to dwell on it. Also, as Johnson well knew, the position he puts to Boswell is founded on the Bible, which helps to explain why he insists on it, more or less as a matter of faith. One difference, however, is that the Bible intrepidly brings us into the areas where Johnson fears to tread — that is, into the sometimes unnerving heart of the paradox itself, with its attendant anxiety and certainty, defiance and submission, lament and protest, terror and elation. In short, the Bible gives us the full roller-coaster ride that Johnson hesitates to take because he knows it will make him dizzy, and he prefers his feet on the ground.

From the beginning, in the opening two chapters of Genesis, the Bible presents us with an interesting contradiction. In Chapter 1, God creates "the heaven and the earth" in six days, and this sequence of events is set out in an orderly fashion. On the sixth day, God introduces his human creation, "man," to rule over the world, thereby completing the design. Chapter 2 tells us in more detail about the creation of Adam and Eve and about the garden of Eden. Adam is created before Eve and is placed in the garden, but God is concerned "that the man should be alone" (2:18), and so he creates the birds and animals, presenting them to Adam "to see what he would call them" (2:19). This contradicts Chapter 1, where the animals are created first, and we might wonder what is going on here.

Medieval commentators tried to get around the difficulty by appealing to 2:5, where God creates "every plant of the field before it was in the earth." This means that God created the seeds first, but, if interpreted through the lens of Greek philosophy, seeds could be taken to mean ideas (God creates the seed of an idea before the actual thing itself). This is a stretch, to say the least, and instead of solving the embarrassing contradiction ends up drawing further attention to it. By contrast, modern Biblical scholars see two stories here from different sources — two strands of tradition brought together by a redactor who held both in such high regard that he let the contradiction stand. Still, the person who put the stories together was not just a slavish copyist but was concerned to present God's truth effectively through the narrative as a whole.

The Biblical scholar and literary critic Robert Alter (*The Art of Biblical Narrative* [*New York: Harper*, 1981]) argues that the redactor presents the creation story in its present form to impress on readers two irreducible truths about our human relationship to God. First, the creation is carefully designed, as Chapter 1 tells us. Second, human beings are created free, and so in Chapter 2 God waits to see how Adam will name the creatures. As Alter says, the keynote in Chapter 1 is "coherence," and in Chapter 2, the fact that Adam is "dangerously free," as the story of the loss of Eden goes on to confirm when Adam eats the forbidden fruit. It might occur to us that in his overly scrupulous hesitation, Sartre's man pondering the menu would have done better at keeping us in Eden than did the over-hasty Adam.

But unlike Sartre, the Bible does not argue about these issues; rather, it presents them as foundational truths, necessary for understanding history itself. The fact of the matter is that God's design is declared by way of agreements or covenants with his people, who are free to transgress. The result of transgression is exile, wandering and suffering; the result of fidelity is rescue, exodus, and a return to peace and prosperity. The interplay between God's plan and human freedom opens, then, upon a further set of key themes pervading the Biblical narratives as a whole, having to do with exodus, covenant, exile, return. The history of Israel is shaped through these interwoven motifs, as is the individual history and self-understanding of each person for whom the Bible is God's truth.

Martin Luther describes the Book of Psalms as a bible within the Bible, by which he means that the main Biblical themes and historical figures are presented there in a compressed form — if we want to see the whole project in miniature, as it were, the Book of Psalms is our best guide. And so I want to comment briefly on how the psalms represent freedom as a dimension of experience in which, paradoxically, we are immersed as part of God's plan. But also, the psalms show us that certain perils attend this view of the world over and above the fact that freedom is risky. These perils are inherent in the dialogue itself between God and his chosen people.

The psalms were composed over several hundred years, beginning perhaps in the tenth century BCE and continuing until the collection as we know it in the Bible was put together in the fifth, or perhaps the fourth, century BCE. Tradition has it that David is the author, but there is broad agreement among scholars that David did not write all of them — a few, maybe, and perhaps none. Inscriptions within the psalms themselves, attributing them to David, are ambiguous and can mean "in the style of" or "appropriate for." Likewise, some psalms are associated with Asaph, the Korahites, Ethan the Ezrahite, among others, though again the exact significance of these attributions is unclear.

The canonical collection has 150 psalms, with slightly different numbers in different versions of the Bible, and with occasional duplications and overlapping. The collection as a whole is made up of several smaller anthologies and is divided into five groups, paralleling the five books of Moses. The breaks are marked by brief prose passages praising God (doxologies), occurring at 41, 72, 89, 106. Psalm 150 does not have a separate doxology, but the whole psalm itself performs this function, rounding off the collection.

Unlike the main Biblical narratives, the psalms are poems, but how they are composed metrically remains unclear. Still, there is broad agreement that parallelism is a basic structural device. That is, brief units of verse parallel one another in rhythm and content, while also introducing small differences counterpointed against the similarities. The result is a rhythmic density which builds dramatic tension through small, incremental contrasts and intensifications. Robert Alter explains these effects in detail in *The Art of Biblical Poetry* (New York: Harper, 1985).

The psalms were used also for liturgical purposes, but many are appropriate for the concerns of individuals, and the corporate voice of Israel does not stand clearly distinct from the supplications, complaints, and laments that an individual person might utter. Throughout, God is praised and remains the all-powerful creator whom we meet in Genesis, separate from the world yet also intimately concerned about it:

When I see Your heavens, the work of Your fingers,
　　the moon and the stars You fixed firm,
"What is man that You should note him,
　　and the human creature, that You pay him heed."
　　　(8:4-5)

Here, God's power brings the heavens into existence, yet even this mighty act is "the work of Your fingers," implying that it is not especially strenuous. "Fingers" also suggests intricate modelling, so that power and intimate concern combine in the contrasting but parallel halves of the line. When the psalmist then turns to "the human creature," the parallel between the heavens and the human confirms the contrast between God's power and our own insignificance. Yet the question, "What is man that You should note him, / and the human creature, that You pay him heed" assumes that God does in fact pay heed, thereby confirming the simultaneous insignificance and special privilege of human beings. The fact that the psalmist puts the question directly to God asserts the high status allowed to humans — a status that the content of the question itself seems to deny. And so the contrast between power and intimate concern in the first two lines is paralleled and reversed in the second two, as we move from great to small and then small to great. These movements in counterpoint are closely bound up with one another and are an example of the interplay between God and "the human creature" which, as we see, is central to the idea of freedom in the Bible as a whole.

The insistence on God's transcendence and intimate care opens readily upon the further idea that God makes agreements with his people, in and through which their freedom is discovered and exercised. That is, God makes binding covenants with the Israelites and gives them laws, as we see especially in the five books of Moses with which the Bible begins. The medium of this exchange between God and humans is, pre-eminently, language, and the Biblical narratives as a whole are heavily laden with dialogue, offsetting a sparseness of pictorial description. The spoken word is foregrounded from the beginning, where God speaks and the creation comes into being. But God's word can also destroy. Thus, he "sends forth His voice and earth melts" (46:7), even though, again, "He sent forth His word and healed them" (107:20). That is, God's word can make or break you, and this same all-powerful, two-edged word binds his people to fidelity. By keeping their word, God's people will prosper; by breaking it, they will suffer. They are free to choose:

> You ordained Your decrees
> > to be strictly observed.
> Would that my ways be firm
> > to observe Your statutes.
> > (119:405)

There is, therefore, a parallel between the creative and destructive power of God's word and the freedom accorded to his people to make or unmake their own happiness and prosperity by obeying or disobeying his decrees. And so God says, "I will not profane My pact / and My mouth's utterance I will not alter" (89:35). But also:

> If his sons forsake My teaching
> > and do not go in my law,
> if they profane My statutes
> > and do not keep My commands,
> I will require their crime with the rod,
> > and with plagues, their wrongdoing.
> > (89:31–33)

That is, God is as good as his word, and his people had better be as good as theirs to avoid disaster. Not surprisingly, the psalmist also asks God to "save my life from lying lips, / from a tongue of deceit" (120:2), by which he means that he seeks protection from slanderers, but also from not keeping his own word. In turn, as the Lord elsewhere says, "Within my house there shall not dwell / one who practices deceit" (101:7). Breaking one's word is, as it were, a de-creative act analogous to the unmaking of the heavens themselves, and it entails a burden of responsibility that is the price of freedom as the Bible understands it.

The stress on fidelity to God's laws by people who are free not to obey has the further important consequence that even the poorest and most destitute will be vindicated if they remain faithful. The Lord "keeps faith forever" and, consequently, "does justice for the oppressed, / gives bread to the hungry, / the Lord looses those in fetters" (146:6–7). This solicitude and concern for the poor and des-titute is a remarkable achievement, both of the psalms and of the Bible elsewhere. And so, throughout the psalms, God's oppressed people cry out to him in distress and even complain that he is not keeping his promises to the suffering faithful. By such means they might change God's mind — after all, God entered into a dialogue with them, and they are free to answer him back, to put their case. Also, when the repentant faithful call out to him, they often do so in the hope that God's power will be directed against Israel's enemies. Indeed, the more distressed and repentant the faithful are, the more justification there is for God directing his anger against the oppres-sors of his people.

Lament, complaint, and longing resonate everywhere in the psalms, reinforcing their urgency and affective power. "My God, my God, why have You forsaken me?" (22:2) — these words, famously spoken (in Aramaic) by Jesus from the Cross, are a cry of desolation, further intensified through the following lines. The anguished cry is uttered first "by day" and then, when there is no answer, "by night." Darkness intensifies the speaker's isolation, which also is a spiritual dark night. In counterpoint, we learn: "In You did our fathers trust, / they trusted, and You set them free" (22:5). But this corporate rescue only emphasizes the speaker's abandonment: "But I am a worm and no man, / a disgrace among men, by the people reviled" (22:7). As a whole, the psalm is a powerful, extended confession of subjection and humiliation before the living God, who is nonetheless praised and invoked, even from the depths of abjection: "Fearers of the Lord, O praise Him!" (22:24).

There are many examples of this kind of lament, sometimes voiced as longing or complaint. "Forgotten from the heart like the dead, / I become like a vessel lost" (31:13); "From the depths I called You, Lord. / Master, hear my voice. / May Your ears listen close to the voice of my plea" (130:1-2). But lament also modulates to indignation at the fact that evil flourishes and the faithful are not vindicated:

> Look, such are the wicked,
>> the ever complacent ones pile up wealth.
> But in vain have I kept my heart pure
>> and in innocence washed my palms.
>>> (73:12-13)

Still, with God's help, the righteous of Israel will triumph, and the flourishing wicked ones will get what they deserve:

> I pursued my enemies, caught them,
>> turned not back till I wiped them out.
> I smashed them, they could not rise,
>> they fell beneath my feet.
> You girt me with might for combat,
>> You laid low my foes beneath me,
> and You made my enemies turn back before me,
>> my foes, I demolished them.
>>> (18:38-41)

That is forthright enough, and the main intent is clear: with God on one's side, the enemy won't stand a chance and will be wiped out. And so the God of armies is invoked frequently (for instance, 46:8; 69:7; 80:5; 84:2), and the psalms can be ferociously vindictive: "Happy who seizes and smashes / your infants against a rock" (137:9); "God, smash their teeth in their mouth" (58:7); "The just man rejoices when vengeance he sees, / his feet he will bathe in the wicked one's blood" (68:11). As God's violence and fury are directed against the unrighteous, God uses Israel's warriors to wreak havoc on his enemies, who are also Israel's.

I once asked an elderly, learned Benedictine monk about those militant psalms, with which he was very familiar because the Book of Psalms is part of the Benedictine office and a selection is read daily. With great patience he explained that the warfare is to be understood spiritually, not literally. This of course is the standard answer for getting around the disturbing violence so plentifully supplied in the holy books of Judaism, Christianity, and Islam alike. But the ease with which such descriptions can be taken to mean what they (literally) say is hard to avoid. The claim that the warfare is spiritual is no doubt sometimes sincere, but in fact the warfare is frequently not spiritual. And that is one of the problems attendant upon believing in a God who makes agreements with a chosen group of people (whether Jews, Christians, or Muslims), calling them to righteousness and giving them freedom. The discovery of autonomous choice for which individuals are responsible and in consequence of which they are answerable to the highest authority is itself a significant human achievement. But, in turn, the highest authority invests true believers with a sense of absolute righteousness, making it easy for them to attack the enemies of the truth imparted specially to them, God's people.

And so we can return to Dr. Johnson's efficient description of freedom. On the one hand, reason tells us that there is a plan (whether God's plan, as Johnson would say, or the necessary chain of cause and effect a materialist would prefer). On the other hand, we know ourselves to be able to make choices. Reason can always claim that such freedom is illusory by appealing to actual, determining conditions, but the fact remains that for practical purposes our experience tells us otherwise. Johnson is right — it won't do to surrender either of the two poles. On the one hand, freedom is not just a disembodied, spontaneous act disconnected from material circumstances — the disembodied nothingness that prevents Sartre's man from choosing his lunch. On the other hand, it is not adequate to regard the human being as an automaton, and in our everyday dealings we treat people as having intentions, options, responsibilities. Rather, freedom is evident in how we are alive and engaged in the world, assessing experience according to certain expectations, standards, and evaluations that are culturally imparted and realized in a unique way by each of us. Consequently, it is important not to lose sight of the uncertainties and tentativeness with which we frequently make our imperfect choices, evaluating and re-evaluating what we think we know and how we ought to behave.

Dr. Johnson understood that freedom is paradoxical, and, at their best, the psalms communicate a richly complex experience of living within the paradox itself. They are celebratory, hopeful, dejected, complaining, confrontational, demanding, confident, doubting, loving, and angry. The urgency, exhilaration, and intensity they impart express the trials, achievements, and tribulations of a people who know that their history is defined by how they exercise their freedom. Yet the psalms show also how freedom might easily turn on itself, begetting its antithesis, namely, violence. Ironically, when it comes to violence, the nihilist and the true believer are likely to have more in common than their professed ideas at first suggest, and Dr. Johnson wasn't far wrong to be apprehensive about both of them.

16

Sex, Society, and Romeo and Juliet

Tragic drama confronts us with an unsettling realization that it is impossible to decide clearly about the part played by human freedom and the part played by fate, or determinism, in bringing about the tragic outcome. This difficulty is compounded when the tragedy is also a love story, because human sexual behaviour is itself a perplexing combination of apparent free choice and unconscious drives that can operate like fate but are also held (partly) in check by social norms, customs, and regulations. Lovers who apparently choose one another freely therefore find themselves enmeshed in the twin determinisms of natural compulsion and social constraint. In turn, we can see this opposition between natural drives and social regulation as corresponding to two main attitudes to erotic love which, for convenience, we can call *anarchic* and *conservative*. The first maintains that love should be free and untrammelled; the second, that it should be responsibly controlled and adapted to the requirements of society.

St. Augustine, who knew all about the conflict between these two attitudes, is a good example of the conservative position. As he tells us in the *Confessions,* he was a compulsive fornicator. The sin that most threatened to consign him to hell, he thought, had to do with sex. As a young man he couldn't contain himself from yielding to the anarchic impulse, and as an old man he wrote conservative treatises on marriage that fairly thrill with hatred for just about everything that the anarchic impulse entails.

Augustine dealt with his demons as Freud says we all do, by repression and sublimation; that is, by keeping the lid on and redirecting the energy in a more or less well-regulated way towards some social or creative enterprise. In Augustine's case, the repression was so strenuous that it provided an all-but-inexhaustible energy, which he deployed especially in explaining church teachings and also in writing about his favourite theme: restlessness. Everywhere, Augustine insists that desire should not be gratified but "referred" to a higher end, God, the single goal and source of love. "Our heart is restless until it rests in Thee," he says, and to search for happiness by way of sensual gratification brings only confusion and pain. And of all the kinds of sensuality preventing us from realizing the one perfect love, sex is the sweetest and also the most poisonous.

In his (once-scandalous) novel, *Tropic of Capricorn,* Henry Miller has his narrator confide that by bitter experience he has learned that what makes the world go round and holds it together is — sexual intercourse. For Miller, a great deal of bitter experience in human affairs arises from sexual repression, from which he was attempting, as a novelist, to relieve us. In so doing, he writes partly in reaction against the conservative mentality cultivated over the centuries by Augustine's brand of Christianity, promoting instead the anarchic alternative. Yet Augustine would be quick to agree that "sexual intercourse" does indeed hold the world together — though he would want to add that this kind of worldliness is precisely the problem. On the same point, Freud (his atheism no hindrance) would concur with the saint. Sex is a main driver in the powerhouse of our turning world.

And again like Augustine, Freud would think that a Henry Miller brand of sexual liberation could only spell disaster, because eros and civilization are interdependent even though also in conflict, as we all are within ourselves. That is, we are sexual because we are human but we are humane because we are civilized and civilization requires the repression of desire.

These days the internet brings us as far along in Miller's anarchic direction as it is perhaps possible to go. Amateurs flaunt, paysites thrive, nothing is denied frontal exposure, sexual organs display their peculiar wonders like creatures brought up from the ocean floor, and people even get addicted. Neither Augustine nor Freud would be surprised. So how do we get it right, this contest between sex and society, eros and the civilized? Let us begin by considering a single line from William Shakespeare's tragic love story, *Romeo and Juliet*.

Near the end of the play, when Romeo and Juliet are already dead in the tomb, a watchman arrives and asks for directions. A frightened pageboy points ahead: "There, where the torch doth burn" (5.3.172). A torch has been placed outside the tomb because Romeo needed to find his way there at night, and so the watchman should go in that direction. Yet, the pageboy says more than he knows, as audiences and readers quickly understand. Insofar as the torch is a beacon indicating the way ahead, it belongs within a series of references throughout the play to navigation, linked in turn to Romeo and Juliet as "star-crossed" lovers. Whether or not they are fated to disaster (their destiny written in the stars) or have navigated badly (their choices caused them to founder) is kept in a carefully unresolved suspension which contributes greatly to the disturbing poignancy of their story. The torch burning bright against a sombre background also reminds us that the young people had shone out against the troubled world of their feuding families. Just as the torch brings illumination to the dark place of the ancestors in the tomb, so Romeo and Juliet's marriage promised to bring new understanding to the feuding houses. But these meanings are now painfully inverted because Romeo and Juliet are in fact dead and their light is extinguished. We are left wondering if they are dead because they were young and foolish (compelled by eros) or because the world of the grownups crushed them with its enmity and greed (civilization taking its toll).

Shakespeare's tragic vision invariably returns us to the core predicament that we see here yet again. That is, we are asked to consider that the qualities for which we most admire a person will, in certain circumstances, bring about that person's destruction. For instance, Hamlet is so thrillingly intelligent that he captivates and dazzles any audience or reader who cares to listen. The bravura performance is of course Shakespeare's, offering to explore the tragic potential of a highly gifted mind and then having to create a poetry that really does express great intellectual distinction. But also, Shakespeare creates a set of circumstances in which Hamlet's high intelligence and powers of analysis are a liability, virtually guaranteeing his demise. The very gifts we admire render him fatally vulnerable in his particular situation.

Another great tragic figure, Othello, offers an exact counter-case. He is an accomplished military leader with a passionate, romantic sensibility expressed in glorious poetry. Provoked by the scheming Iago, he becomes pathologically jealous and murders his innocent wife. Everything depends on Iago preventing Othello from pausing to analyze the situation, and if Othello and Hamlet were to change places, each finding himself in the other's situation, there would be no tragic endings. Othello — decisive and effective, a man of action — would not hesitate but would confront the murderous Claudius. Hamlet — introverted, analytical — would take his time and easily see through the monstrous Iago. In short, Othello's tragedy is that he does not hesitate, and Hamlet's is that he does, and Shakespeare imagines a set of circumstances in which hesitation on the one hand and precipitate action on the other are irreparably destructive.

Yet, within each play, circumstance and character also remain so interwoven that we cannot simply moralize (the tragedy is caused by personal weakness) or simply resort to fatalism (circumstances alone are to blame). The tragic fact is that gifted and admirable human beings can be destroyed because of their gifts, and where is the justice in that? Shakespeare doesn't say, but if we cannot admire and have compassion for the heroes, then Shakespeare's poetry fails; if we do not feel defiant about the cruelties of fate, mediated by society and its impersonal constraints, then we do not grasp how vulnerable even the most gifted people really are.

Romeo and Juliet is not quite a tragedy on the scale of *Hamlet* and *Othello*, but the same central predicament governs the play. From the start, the youngsters are circumstanced by the hatred between their families and by old Capulet's financial need to marry off his daughter, Juliet, to a rich young count. We quickly feel that there is no way out, and the Chorus, addressing us in the Prologue before the play begins, tells us just that. The "ancient grudge" of the feud prevails, and from "the fatal loins of these two foes / A pair of star-crossed lovers take their life." Already, we feel an unsettling ambivalence: "take their life" means that they are born into this world from the "loins" of the two families, but the words also intimate their joint suicide. The Chorus then informs us that they do indeed die, and that the play will show their "misadventured piteous overthrows" and the "fearful passage of their death-marked love." "Misadventured" suggests that they are partly to blame, that they were rash to act as they did. "Star-crossed" puts the opposite case: the fates were against them. And so the chorus does not just set the scene for us in "fair Verona" but confronts us with the central, tragic conundrum, asking us to have compassion for the "piteous overthrows" that follow upon misadventure, and also to ponder the "fearful" workings of the social codes that weigh on the young people's lives like fate.

No doubt, the youngsters are rash, impetuous, so suddenly intense and impatient that we feel their immense vulnerability and would be inclined to warn them off. Unerringly as ever, Shakespeare allows such a caution to be voiced within the play, not by the discredited elders of the feuding families but by Romeo's wittily cynical friend Mercutio. With immense verve, the (mercurial) Mercutio mocks at

Romeo's romantic excess (this especially *before* Romeo meets Juliet), and in a famous set piece he describes for Romeo (and for us) the seductions of imagination, which he sees as the province of the fairy Queen Mab and her helpers.

Mercutio describes an attractive miniature world in which Mab's chariot is a hazelnut shell driven by a "gray-coated gnat" (1.4.64) and built from spider-legs and the wings of grasshoppers. Things hover on the edge of insubstantiality, shot through with a glimmer of moonshine, and from here the fairies produce dreams and wishful fantasies in the minds of humans. Mercutio is delighted with himself, using imagination to depict how imagination works. His language moves lightly, designed to keep the topic playfully in perspective, under control, even though towards the end the fairy dreams take a disturbing turn and Mab becomes sinister. Still, Mercutio remains deft and the speech continues to amuse, its darker touches kept also at a wry distance. But for all his verve and brilliance, Mercutio speaks in the end for the conservative position.

Romeo has something to learn here. A touch of humour and some perspective on his own emotional excesses would help him to set his feet more firmly on the ground. Still, Mercutio's persistent bawdiness (he has the dirtiest mind of all the principals) and a nasty edge to his cynicism cause us, in turn, not to embrace him wholeheartedly. We grant him his point and he is fun, but all in all he is cheap in comparison to the young lovers, reckless and anarchic as they are.

More than any other character in the play, Mercutio comes from the world of Shakespeare's comedies, and it is a critical cliché to notice that *Romeo and Juliet* begins like a comedy and then turns tragic. At the start, the elegant milieu, the contest between old parents and young lovers, the wit, extravagance, and brilliance of the masked ball with the bustle of servants and musicians, the love rivalries and high romantic artifice, the swift, buoyant tempo — all this is filled with the promise of comedy. But comedy dies when Mercutio is killed, and the play quickly swerves into a dark and sombre, different kind of world.

And so at the start, we see Romeo and Juliet as part of a bustling, brilliant community, and even the inter-family feud seems on the brink of being repaired. But as tragedy closes around them, this sense of community is replaced by isolation. They become introverted, secretive, haunted by bad dreams and premonitions, having to conceal their marriage as their high-risk behaviour forces them into a dangerous solitariness, separated from one another when Romeo is banished to Mantua after killing Tybalt in revenge for Mercutio's death. Comedy is always about community, and tragedy about isolation; *Romeo and Juliet* shows the two kinds within a single play, moving from one to the other.

The poetry Shakespeare gives his young lovers is at its most affecting as the tragic sense deepens. Ecstatic love-longing, anguish, fear, hope, and erotic intensity shot through with intimations of death hold us within the experience itself of sexuality alive yet confined, exigent yet thwarted, beautiful yet condemned. Here, for instance, is Romeo in Mantua, separated from Juliet and awakening from a dream of her:

> If I may trust the flattering truth of sleep,
> My dreams presage some joyful news at hand.
> My bosom's lord sits lightly in his throne,
> And all this day an unaccustomed spirit
> Lifts me above the ground with cheerful thoughts.
> I dreamt my lady came and found me dead
> (Strange dream that gives a dead man leave to think!)
> And breathed such life with kisses in my lips
> That I revived and was an emperor.
> Ah me! How sweet is love itself possessed,
> When but love's shadows are so rich in joy!
> (5.1.1–11)

He is flushed with optimism, a sense that all will be well and that the dream (unlike many other premonitions in the play) is a good omen, a bringer of "joyful news." The troubadour buoyancy of "my bosom's lord sits lightly in his throne" gives us the feel of Romeo's lightheartedness, and the welcome relief of the "cheerful thoughts" is elating, as if he is walking on air. Yet, from the first line a countercurrent also runs against the elated mood. Because the truth of sleep might be "flattering," he wonders if he can trust it, but then this momentary hesitation yields quickly to the dream of his lady kissing him back to life. Still, even this dream contains a further, unsettling dimension. Juliet has found him dead before her kisses revive him, and Romeo pauses to wonder at the contrary elements ("Strange dream that gives a dead man leave to think"). We begin to feel that his hope for a happy ending (the play as comedy) is already undermined by a less consciously acknowledged unease (the intimation of tragedy). After all, it takes a fairy-tale miracle to restore him as "emperor," the prince brought back to life by a fairy princess, a sort of reversal of *Sleeping Beauty*. The last line, declaring how sweet love is when even its "shadows" (or dreams) are "so rich in joy" is ambivalent. It can mean that the real thing is better than our dreams and imaginings, but also that we are led on by shadows which are illusions, offering a "flattering truth" against which reality fails to measure up. The combination of eager hope, nervous tension, danger, joy, and the deceptions of imagination is held here, miraculously agile and elegant, between hope and fear, alive with longing and passionate intensity. And of course it is all destroyed. A few lines later, when Romeo is informed (misinformed, in fact) that Juliet is dead, he prepares to rush back to Verona, the city from which he is banished on pain of death. Eros and civilization stand now uncompromisingly opposed. "I defy you, stars!" Romeo says, and the messenger, Balthasar, asks him to "have patience," noticing that his looks are "pale and wild" and "do import some misadventure." And so we return to the fated, "star-crossed" theme and the question of responsibility, "misadventure," and bad navigation.

As we see, Shakespeare is not uncritical of the young people's rash excess, and there is something daft in all this adolescent intensity. Yet the poetry he provides for Romeo and Juliet holds us enthralled, and when they are dead we feel pathos and also contempt for the failures and blindness of the adult world that could not do better for them. As an exercise in complexity of tone, *Romeo and Juliet* is unsurpassed, and we might see something of this, again, in the line with which I began: "There, where the torch burns bright." Almost a throwaway, spoken by the most minor of minor characters, it gathers to itself and opens out upon a set of meanings together with their ironic inversions, knit into the play's whole substance and texture.

Nothing less than complexities like this will show us the issue well enough — the idealizing aspirations and constraints that inspire and confine erotic desire, the disconcerting combination of romantic ecstasy and impetuous foolishness, the narcissism that is also selfless, the brilliance that does not endure but remains all the more haunting. Beside all this, the theological stringency of the beetling Augustine, like the quasi-mechanisms of Freudian repression and sublimation and the strident Milleresque freedoms of the supposedly liberated, appear thin, mere formal impositions upon the vital power and our attempts to manage it.

And without exception we manage it imperfectly. As a rite of passage to a conscionable humanity, everyone needs to encounter some version of star-crossed circumstances requiring the sacrifice of passionate intensity and calling for decisions beyond the scope of reason. Shakespeare does not decide such personal matters for us, but lets us understand what such decisions are about. Meanwhile, people by and large do what they can, defying the principled naysayers while keeping a lid on destructive excess, muddling along in the half-light of an uncertain freedom, for the most part in the realm of tragicomedy, wishing that things were otherwise.

17

Cartoons from Denmark and the March of the Zombies

What are the limits to freedom of speech and of expression? Are blasphemy laws ever a good idea, and what about incitement to hatred? Should anyone ever be killed for what he or she says or writes? These questions have taken on a pressing significance in recent years, beginning, perhaps, with the fatwa against Salman Rushdie because of his novel *The Satanic Verses*. At the time, the threat against Rushdie, and the offering of a reward to his killer, seemed anomalous. But it might well have been a harbinger of things to come — as, for instance, the more recent controversy and outrage over a set of cartoons from Denmark suggests.

In 2005, the Danish newspaper *Jyllands-Posten* published twelve cartoons, some of which depicted the prophet Muhammad. Predictably, a good many of the faithful were not in the mood for satire and saw mainly blasphemy and contempt. In frustration and anger, a group of Danish imams prepared a dossier and took to the road on a sort of anti-pilgrimage, displaying the unholy objects across the Middle East.

Somewhere along the line, three further pictures were added to the original twelve and were passed off as the work of the iniquitous newspaper, although in fact they were not. One of these extra items was a photograph of a man in a beard, wearing a false pig's snout. As it happens, he was a participant in a pig-squealing contest at a French country fair and had nothing to do either with Muhammad or the cartoons. In the same enterprising spirit, the false claim was also put about that *Jyllands-Posten* was a state-run newspaper and that the Danish government was therefore responsible. It didn't take long for yet a further embellishment to fill out the picture: the cartoons, we were to know, originated in the United States, and *Jyllands-Posten* was merely delivering Uncle Sam's message.

Well juiced on grievance and rumour, a protest movement in Denmark rapidly bulked up, and in 2006, a road-rage of violence broke out across the globe. By the end of March, at least 139 people had been killed, mostly in Nigeria, Libya, Pakistan, and Afghanistan. In Syria, the Norwegian and Danish embassies were burned, as were the Italian embassy in Libya, the Dutch embassy in Beirut and the Austrian embassy in Tehran. In Turkey, an Italian Catholic priest was murdered, as was a sixty-seven-year-old Coptic man in Egypt. In both cases, the assassins said the cartoons were the cause.

Death threats, street riots, rewards promised for decapitation, official complaints from ambassadors, economic boycotts, and worldwide protests came so thick and fast as to evoke incredulity: all this can't be, surely, about *cartoons?* Well, of course, there is more to it, but, yes, these tasteless drawings really were such an affront that they left no doubt in the minds of some of the offended about what exactly should be done. This became all too clear, for instance, in placards displayed at a march to the Danish embassy in London on 3 February 2006: "Slay those who insult Islam"; "Butcher those who mock Islam"; "Behead those who insult Islam"; "Exterminate those who slander

Islam"; "Massacre those who insult Islam." Then, upping the ante: "Europe you will pay. Your extermination is on its way"; "Europe is the cancer; Islam is the answer"; "Be prepared for the *Real* holocaust." And, as if to summarize the case: "Freedom go to hell."

A great many Muslims were (and remain) bewildered and upset by such extremism. In Denmark, an MP, Naser Khader, organized a Muslim group to provide a counterweight to the inflammatory imams. In England, Asghar Bukhari, chair of the Muslim Affairs Committee, argued that the London demonstration of 3 February should have been stopped because of the violence advocated by some marchers. It is not hard to imagine a broad spectrum of Muslim response along such lines, and it is not difficult either to sympathize with Muslims who feel offended by the drawings. Their reasons are understandable and can readily be shared. But the indulgence in rage and violence, costing people their lives, is grotesque. If killing is permitted because of an insult, then it is easy to interpret dissent itself as an insult to be treated accordingly. Soon there is no end to the discovery of any number of insults, real or implied, linked by a chain of guilt by association, as with the violence which spread across the globe from Denmark. The Tunisian human rights activist Abu Khawla soberly reminds us that "fighting infidels until they either convert to Islam or submit to Muslims as 'Dhimmis' . . . is still considered by Islamists to be a religious duty." Although countless Muslims are not "Islamists" in this sense, some are, and they have given notice.

At this point it is worth recalling that Muslims are not alone in their conviction that they are the chosen guardians of a religious truth to which others ought to submit. In general, Judaism, Christianity, and Islam share a similarly rigorous view of the difference between insiders and outsiders — the saved and the damned. Those who enjoy access to God's truth are separated absolutely from the others with whom God, sitting in judgment, will deal harshly because they have turned away from him. Some softening of this obdurate exclusivism is provided by exegetes who remind us that while we are on earth it is not clear who is holy in God's eyes and who is not.

Consequently, we ought not to rush to judgment, and during our earthly sojourn we should engage ourselves in a mainly spiritual warfare against the forces of evil, leaving the final distribution of punishments to the Almighty. But all too frequently it has seemed very clear indeed who on earth is unholy, blasphemous, and idolatrous, and the histories of the People of the Book present us with an appalling amount of violence inflicted in God's name.

The fierce monotheisms of the Middle East have much to answer for, but here I am concerned with the youngest of them, whose main holy book, the Qur'an, insists relentlessly on the opposition between believers and unbelievers. "Those who reject Faith, / And die rejecting — / On them is Allah's curse /. . . ./ Their penalty will not / Be lightened, nor will / Respite be their (lot)" (2:161–62); "Those who reject / Our Signs, We shall soon / Cast into the fire" (4:56); "Those who reject faith /. . . ./ Will be Companions / Of Hell-fire" (5:10); "the Unbelievers will be / Gathered together to Hell" (8:36); "Those who reject the Book /. . . ./ They shall be dragged along — / In the boiling fetid fluid; / Then in the Fire / Shall they be burned" (40:70–72). Also, "Unbelievers are / Unto you open enemies" (4:101); "O ye who believe! ·Fight / The Unbelievers who gird you about" (9:123); "Muhammad is the Messenger / Of Allah; and those who are / With him are strong / Against Unbelievers, (but) / Compassionate amongst each other" (48:29). "Unbelievers" who "desist (from Unbelief)" will be forgiven; otherwise "fight them" until "there prevails / Justice and faith in Allah" (8:39). At the last judgment, "those who have rejected / Faith" will "be brought forth to Punishment" (30:16), whereas the faithful "Shall be made happy / In a Mead of Delight" (30:15). Meanwhile, "when the forbidden months / Are past, then fight and slay / The Pagans wherever ye find them, / And seize them, beleaguer them, / And lie in wait for them / In every stratagem (of war)" (9:5).

Interpreters might insist that injunctions to warfare such as the above are mainly spiritual, a calling for a greater holy war against sinful self-indulgence rather than the lesser, tragic warfare involving actual violence. Also, the sheer severity of the threatening language can bring home to individual believers that their responsibilities are of the highest seriousness. Conducting themselves accordingly, many Muslims find in the complex traditions developing from the Qur'an, the hadiths, and sharia a peaceful means for organizing their personal lives. But for the moment I am concerned to notice how passages such as those I have cited can make it easy for sufficiently aggrieved believers to construe the call to arms in material terms. One result is that various radical factions pursue a violent agenda in the name of religion (which they do not adequately understand) such as Europe has not experienced in modern times, and which appears today as threatening and bizarre as the Danish cartoon furor, its image in miniature.

Nobel laureate Elias Canetti can help us to understand some further dimensions of this unsettling phenomenon. Canetti writes well about crowds (*Crowds and Power* [New York: Continuum, 1973]). He notices that invisible crowds are important in all religions, "but in Islam, more strongly than in any of the other world religions, there are invisible *double* crowds standing in opposition to one another" (141). Canetti points out that the final "double crowd of the Last Judgement is prefigured in every earthly battle" (142); that is, the invisible (spiritual, let us say) is imaged forth in the visible (material) reality of actual day-to-day struggles against the unbelievers, mockers, and blasphemers. Consequently, when an offence is judged egregious, there is a strong incentive to deal with it here and now as God will surely do by and by. "Slay the idolaters," says the Qur'an; "slay those who insult Islam," says the placard. Peace-loving pieties notwithstanding, the barrier between the visible crowd and the invisible is perilously indistinct, not least because we will all be dead by and by, and so we are already a virtual part of the invisible crowd of all who have lived before us. Ask any aspiring suicide bomber: paradise — and the blessed host who dwell there (our crowd) — are a mere step away, a hair-trigger of separation.

Still, the happy crowd in paradise is a far cry from the murderous gangs roaming the streets, ready to kill anyone who could be taken to represent, by proxy, the blasphemous cartoonists. In such a situation, revenge does not require any actual culprit to be identified and held responsible; rather, anyone belonging to and therefore *representing* the community of which the culprit is a member will do. This principle of "representative identity," as the political scientist Frank Wright tellingly calls it, and to which I have referred in earlier chapters, is evident in every modern ethnic conflict zone, and is deeply rooted in an archaic human need to preserve group solidarity against an outside threat. If the group does not survive, neither does the individual, and when the group is threatened, individual judgment must yield to the task of repelling the common enemy, who, in turn, is represented by anyone deemed to be a member of the outside crowd. As Canetti says, the surrender of individual responsibility, of individual space, is one main gratification of joining a crowd, of jostling and rubbing shoulders, being carried along rather than standing apart and thinking for yourself. And so the mechanisms of a quasi-tribal retribution, fired by a transcendent claim for a pure and perfect justice, are directed against the cartoonists and anyone who might be taken to support the values informing their insulting behaviour. More or less randomly chosen individuals — such as the two unfortunates in Turkey and Egypt — will do, as might anyone whose failure to belong with the right crowd is taken to constitute a rejection of the one truth that matters.

Yet the appeal of secular common sense against religious extremism can also be a deceptively convenient salve for the consciences of those who make it. Political grievances underlie much of the murderous resentment driving the violent "Islamist" radicalism outlined by Abu Khawla, and it is often easier to denounce religious fanaticism than to put the dirty politics in the limelight. Tariq Ali, for one, regrets the energy wasted on the cartoons controversy and wishes that more attention had been focused on Iraq and Palestine. The violently-minded placard carriers would have done better to curtail their excesses not just because these are reprehensible (which they are) but because their own best interests would be served if they were not so embarrassingly fixated on reviving an anachronism — the old theocratic zombie stirred up, a stultified automaton again lurching around on the rampage.

For Thomas Browne (1605–82), the wars of seventeenth-century Europe provided an all-too-bitter example of religion deployed in the service of violence. In light of this experience, Browne worries (especially) that people are too ready to be sure of themselves on questions pertaining to the mysteries of existence, seeking security in dogma rather than exercising the more difficult freedom of critical thought. As he reminds us, "no man knows himself"; also, as a corollary, "no man knows another" (73), and such imperfect understanding is a poor foundation on which to proclaim certainty about the meaning of everything — especially the kind of religious certainty that condemns to hell all those who don't agree. Yet, as Canetti says, the opaque and tremulous self feels stronger in a crowd, and a newly discovered self-importance then can masquerade as humility — a sense of being unworthy but chosen for a high cause of such absolute import that in its service others might be demonized, scapegoated, and worse. Inflation of such an order is especially vulnerable to satire, as many thinkers in the age of Browne have shown, to our lasting benefit. Browne — himself a believer — preferred to be a genial rather than a caustic satirist, putting the case for moderation, freedom of critical enquiry, and the avoidance of harm. It isn't such a bad position to recommend, but neither is it surprising that in awakening us to it, satire itself might be all the more intensely resented.

Vergil and the Almighty Dollar

No country on earth proclaims itself the defender of freedom ("leader of the free world") as emphatically as does the United States of America. But the freedom which is often imagined in ideal terms as God's special mandate to his favoured custodian is in fact closely tied to and exercised by means of those two basic instruments of force: money and military power. Free citizens exercising their capacities to the full within a society that respects equality and individual difference is an ideal not likely to be realized today any more than it was at the beginning of speculation on the topic in Plato's time. But it is helpful to acknowledge the contradictions between the ideal and the actual, and to understand that freedom that is bought or enforced is a parody of the real thing.

As it happens, the US one-dollar bill, so readily to hand, illustrates the four points I have just mentioned: state power, money, freedom, God. The dollar bill is, as it were, a small text, though not often (one imagines) closely read. Let us dwell a little on some details, beginning with the Great Seal.

The Great Seal of the United States is used for official purposes and is held for safekeeping by the secretary of state. Also, it is reproduced on the back of the one-dollar bill — the foundation document (as it were) against which the world's currencies by and large measure their worth. In turn, the dollar is backed by the world's most powerful state apparatus, and, as the Great Seal reminds us, the state defends the values of the new age initiated by the founding fathers who came up with the idea of a Great Seal in the first place: Benjamin Franklin, John Adams, and Thomas Jefferson.

After three committees had deliberated over the course of six years, a design for the Great Seal was agreed upon in 1782. Secretary of Congress Charles Thomson oversaw the final proceedings and offered Congress an explanation. The pyramid on the reverse of the seal signifies "strength and duration," and the eye and motto, *annuit coeptis,* "allude to the many signal interpositions of providence in favour of the American cause." The motto under the pyramid, *novus ordo seclorum,* and the date, MDCCLXXVI (1776), "signify the beginnings of the new American Aera, which commences from that date." On the front of the seal, the thirteen stars and the motto, *e pluribus unum,* signify "the several states all joined in one solid compact entire" (there were thirteen states at the time). Other details featuring the number 13 also fit with Thomson's explanation. The eagle with its wings spread beneath the thirteen stars holds thirteen arrows in its left talon and an olive branch with thirteen leaves and thirteen buds in its right. The eagle represents state power, and chooses peace or war at its own discretion.

The motto above the pyramid, *annuit coeptis* ("he has prospered our undertakings"), is from Vergil's *Aeneid* 9.625 (with perhaps an allusion to the *Georgics,* 1.40). Vergil's (70–19 BCE) great epic poem, the *Aeneid,* celebrates the imperial might of ancient Rome, and was written for the emperor Augustus, who consolidated Roman state power after a bitter civil war. The motto below the pyramid, *incipit novus ordo seclorum* ("a new order of the ages begins") derives from Vergil's Fourth Eclogue, a short poem which prophetically heralds a new golden age.

As Thomson says, the eye and the words, *annuit coeptis,* indicate providence — that is, God's design. It is easy to understand how the eye suggests all-seeing watchfulness, but it is less easy to see how Vergil fits in. In the *Aeneid,* the words of the motto are spoken by Ascanius, the immature and reckless son of the hero, Aeneas. Ascanius asks Jove for help, and uses an imperative form of the verb (*annue*). Soon after, Ascanius is placed under the protection of Apollo. Thomson changes the verb to the past tense (*annuit*), so that the request becomes an established fact. That is, providence (rather than Jove) has already approved and watched over the undertakings described in the motto below, announcing the "new order of the ages." In turn, as we see, this phrase derives from Vergil's *Fourth Eclogue,* in which the poet celebrates the birth of a divine child who will bring in a new golden age. Vergil again flatters the Emperor, though he does not name him. (The poet was hedging his bets until the civil war was over; whoever won would then be praised as the father of the wonder child. As it turns out, Augustus was victorious.) Also, Vergil further protects himself by attributing the prophecy to a Sibylline Oracle.

Here we might notice that the divine providence described by Thomson derives from Christianity and is therefore incompatible with Vergil's polytheism. Yet this is an old problem, and during the Middle Ages a great deal of effort went into making Vergil a sort of proto-Christian. For instance, early Christian commentators interpreted the Fourth Eclogue as a prophecy about the birth of Jesus. Vergil was therefore held to be inspired by the Biblical God, and was interpreted as a bridge between ancient Rome and the new Holy Roman Empire, which used the administrative and legal apparatus, roads, and (eventually) the armed forces of the ancient empire to extend Christ's redemptive message to sinners everywhere.

The fourth-century historian, Eusebius, reports that Constantine, the first Christian Emperor, addressed an ecclesiastical assembly and said flat out that in the *Fourth Eclogue* Vergil knew he was foretelling the birth of Christ but concealed the message to avoid provoking the authorities. After Constantine, Vergil enjoyed a special status as the one illustrious pagan who was, as it were, an honorary Christian, and a great deal of effort went into making the *Aeneid* into good reading for the orthodox. This was achieved mainly by way of allegory: that is, episodes in the *Aeneid* were interpreted as colourful stories showing forth a higher, Christian truth. The results are often forced and arbitrary to the point of silliness, as a brief glance at the sixth-century commentary by Fabius Planciades Fulgentius, *De Continentia Virgiliana,* quickly shows. But why such an expense of labour, such egregious special pleading?

As a way of approaching an answer, I would like to detour briefly by way of the resurrection stories in the gospels. It is now widely accepted that Mark's gospel ends at 16:8 and that the remaining brief section, 16:9–20, was added by another hand. This means that Mark has no resurrection appearances and therefore does not distinguish between the resurrection and the *parousia* (second coming). Mark is full of apocalyptic anxieties and expectations, and his gospel leaves us feeling that Jesus's resurrection and the end times might well be the same event. Also, Mark has no birth story.

Matthew and Luke add quite elaborate birth stories and, to match them, similarly elaborate resurrection stories. In doing so, they address the fact that the end times are not yet upon us, and a special "time of Jesus" has occurred within history — which is to say, Jesus was born and died and was resurrected. He then ascended to heaven and we will have to wait for him to return at the end times. The gap between Jesus's return to his Father in heaven and his coming again is the time of Christian history, which will end in due course (as the luridly violent Book of Revelation promises). Meanwhile, Christians should live their lives faithfully, announcing the good news and preparing themselves and others for the final event. To do this effectively, early Christians set about organizing a Christian state. Rome provided the infrastructure, and the most powerful celebration of

the virtues of the empire at the height of its glory is Vergil's *Aeneid.*
Constantine did what he could to make Vergil's vision of Rome the
model upon which Christian history would be shaped in the wait-
ing period between Jesus's leaving the world and his return to it. The
empire would be the first to welcome him back, confounding its enemies (who are his enemies too) in the process.

To a surprising degree, the core ideas and expectations about
Christian history that I have just described remain durable in the
new American "order of the ages." Although the separation of church
and state is declared in the Constitution, the Enlightenment heritage that privileges reason, secular politics, and human rights in
the United States remains uneasily related to the Puritan heritage
emphasizing the community of a chosen people, the elect guided by
God. Certainly, presidents aren't shy about invoking providence. In
his inaugural address, Barack Obama confides that "the source of
our confidence" is "the knowledge that God calls on us to shape an
uncertain destiny." And at the 51st Prayer Breakfast (what are we to
make of *that* institution?) in February 2003, George W. Bush reminds
his audience that Americans "can be confident in the ways of Providence, even when they are far from our understanding." And so, not
surprisingly, on the back of the dollar bill the words "In God We
Trust" are printed in the centre, directly above the number "One."
The number indicates the value of the bill (the secular sense) while
also declaring a (non-secular) trust in the One God.

On the right of the number One, the front side of the Great Seal
features the eagle. As we see, its hands are full, and so its beak is
used to hold a banner with the words *e pluribus unum* ("from many,
one"). The motto indicates how one nation is made from the thirteen states, and is often taken to mean also that the United States is
a melting pot, an immigrant nation made up of many components.
Yet an intriguing subtext links the "one" of the motto, the One God,
and the single eye in the triangle (the reverse side of the seal, printed
to the left of the number, One). As we have seen, the eye represents
providence — God's eternal watchfulness. The pyramid has thirteen

layers and, together with the eye, reproduces the idea of the single nation made from thirteen states. The eye in the triangle is separate from the pyramid (there is a gap between them), but it also completes the design by forming the apex. The eye inside a triangle might also suggest the One God who is paradoxically single yet threefold — another version of *e pluribus unum,* this time not so secular.

The eagle holding the olives and arrows is the American bald eagle, but to have chosen an eagle in the first place (Benjamin Franklin wanted a rattlesnake) is unmistakably to evoke the imperial eagle of ancient Rome — a main symbol of the might of empire. As we have seen, the arrows and olive branch represent the alternatives that empires always offer — peace or war. Typically, peace is on the terms declared by those who have power, and if you don't take the olives you will have to face the arrows (missiles, that is). And so it was also with the so-called "pax Augusta" declared by the emperor Augustus and celebrated by Vergil. But Vergil well knew the tragic cost of the exercise of state power required to bring peace about; he knew, and lamented, that pacification and peace are not the same.

In the *Aeneid,* Vergil tells the story of the remote foundation of Rome. The hero, Aeneas, escapes after Troy is besieged and destroyed by the Greeks. Aeneas flees with a band of survivors, and the first half of Vergil's twelve-book poem tells of Aeneas's travels and adventures as he seeks the land where he will found the dynasty that will eventually become the Rome of Augustus Caesar. The second half of the poem tells about Aeneas's landing in Italy and the wars he fought there to establish a seat of power, find a wife, and pacify the tribes that threatened peace — again, much as Augustus was to do.

The *Aeneid* is highly sophisticated, and among other things Vergil reinterprets Homer's great epics, appropriating them to the Roman cause. Thus, the first half of the *Aeneid* can be read as a version of the *Odyssey* (adventures and trials) and the second half, of the *Iliad* (war and its outcome). By such means, Vergil allows the glories of Greece to enhance the grandeur of Rome, and Augustus was no doubt pleased. But the *Aeneid* also registers a poignant understanding of the human tragedy that attends the triumphs of empire. There are many ways to show this, but here I want briefly to notice Vergil's ironic treatment of violence — a disturbing counterpoint to the heroic display, the official compliment to Augustus and the *Pax Romana*.

From the start, Vergil has a problem, in that his hero, Aeneas, is already defeated, fleeing from Troy and from the victorious Greeks. Throughout the *Aeneid* we watch his slow rehabilitation, and one of Vergil's main achievements is to show how Aeneas's character develops as the poem progresses. In counterpoint, Vergil provides information on some key figures among the victorious Greeks. For instance, the triumphant Pyrrhus comes to a bad end (3.333), and when King Latinus sends envoys to the Greek hero Diomedes to ask for help against Aeneas's forces, Diomedes refuses, explaining that the Greeks have "paid frightful price and penalty" for their victory at Troy. He goes on to list their misfortunes, naming Menelaus, Ulysses, Neoptolemus [Pyrrhus], Idomeneus, and Agamemnon (11.258ff). It is tempting to see this as Vergil's way of playing down the Greek victory in order to boost Aeneas. But the idea that military victories in general are not as heroic as they might seem runs throughout the *Aeneid* as a powerful counter-message to the official celebration of military prowess. The truth is, violence is unpredictable and depersonalizing. Friend and foe become alike until the laws of force play themselves out. Also, violence has a way of turning on itself so that in hunting down your victim you might actually be hunting yourself down without knowing it.

There is a great deal about hunting in the *Aeneid,* and its main relevance lies in how it pertains to Vergil's treatment of war. Like war, hunting is a violent behaviour shaped and governed by rules and rituals which attempt to civilize it, making it seem like a sport. Just as a hunter is said to "dress" a kill, ritually sanitizing the butchery, so, analogously, in the *Aeneid* frequent attention is paid to dressing up in arms and armour and despoiling the dead enemy in a sort of ritual triumphalism. In the interplay between war as a sport or ritual display and the actual horror and confusions of violence, Vergil develops a characteristic, poignant but fierce irony. A couple of examples will suffice.

In Book 2, Aeneas recounts the final destruction of Troy. Foolishly, the Trojans breach their own walls and bring in the wooden horse left outside by the Greeks, supposedly as a peace offering to Pallas. The Greeks then pretend to lift the siege and return home. But at night the soldiers concealed inside the horse "fell on a city buried in sleep and wine" (2.265) and threw open the gates to admit their companions. The flames of the burning city provide a lurid half-light in which the identities of friend and foe are confused and blind terror reigns. The ghost of Hector warns Aeneas to flee (2.289), but Aeneas takes up arms, wanting to die heroically — "like a fool I seized my sword"; "'Glory!' I thought, 'to die in battle!'" (2.317). His followers, their "mad young hearts" fired up, are "like wolves / driven by horrid belly lust" (2.357) as terror and fury take over until "dead men lay by thousands" (2.364). In the mayhem, a group of Greeks mistake the Trojans for friends, and these Trojans seize the opportunity and kill the Greeks. Then Coroebus has a bright idea and suggests that the Trojans dress in Greek armour and use the disguise to hunt down other Greeks. This works well initially, until some Trojans mistake their disguised friends for enemies, and Trojan starts killing Trojan. And so violence obliterates the differences between friend and foe, as heroism descends into blood lust. A clever stratagem is turned on its head, and the hunters are hunted.

The death of the warrior maiden Camilla in Book 11 provides a further example of how Vergil means us to see this same process. Camilla leads her Volscian warriors in support of Turnus, who is Aeneas's chief enemy in the second half of the poem. Camilla is an engaging and glamorous figure, full of high spirits as she leaps from her horse to join Turnus in a plot to ambush Aeneas. She is protected by the goddess Diana, who promises to avenge any harm done to her and who instructs the nymph, Opis, to guard Camilla and to kill anyone who harms her.

When the fighting starts, Camilla slaughters her enemies wholesale, but the wily Arruns tracks her down — "Houndlike, he circled her" — as Vergil again deploys the hunting motif to describe the strategy. Camilla then makes a fatal mistake. She spots the flashy, brilliantly armed Chloreus and singles him out to kill him so that she can take his armour, both for display and to "dress herself — for hunting" (11.778). While Camilla pauses to despoil the dead Chloreus, Arruns takes his chance and, in turn, kills her. But then Arruns also indulges in the heroic glory of the moment, and Diana's sentinel, Opis, finds him "all glittering arms and foolish pride" (11.854) and, in turn, kills him.

This episode develops the implications of those fatal disguises the Trojans assumed to stalk the Greeks in Book 2. Here, Arruns tracks down Camilla and succeeds in killing her, but he is unwitting in that in so doing he also stalks himself. Ironically, he seals his own fate at the very moment when he thinks he is victorious. His situation mirrors Camilla's, and he is hunted even as he hunts, proudly dressed in glittering armour to signify a triumph which in fact is a defeat. Victor and victim resemble one another, and the circle of violence returns to destroy the perpetrator — as the victorious Greeks themselves discovered after their victory at Troy. All of which helps to explain the painful complexity of the episode with which the *Aeneid* ends.

In Book 12, after an elaborate chase that again evokes the hunting motif, Aeneas defeats Turnus and holds him at swordpoint. Turnus capitulates and Aeneas checks the fatal blow — "his eye wavered, he halted" (12.939). But then Aeneas notices that Turnus is dressed in the armour of the boy Pallas, Aeneas's favourite whom Turnus had killed in a frenzy of triumphalist violence. Aeneas feels "a flame of fury and dreadful rage" (12.946) flare up within him, and he strikes the disarmed and suppliant Turnus dead.

Again, Turnus is killed because he has killed, and his heroic self-glorification in despoiling Pallas of his armour signs his own death warrant. But although Aeneas is at last triumphant, Vergil leaves us with a resonating bitterness and sadness. As he well knew, the order imposed by state power contains and suppresses whatever violence would prevent the work of civilization. Yet he knew also that the mere tranquilizing of force-relationships is not peace but a parody of peace, and those who impose their will by violence are sowing the seeds of the violence that will be turned against them. Heraldic display, heroic posturing, and confidence in divine appointment merely conceal this difficult realization.

The *Aeneid* shows how attractive such heroic concealments can be — and also how dangerous. By contrast, the Great Seal gives us the heroic facade glossed over with a dressing of religion, but without any sense of the pathos on which the old pagan poet insists. Of course we do not expect to discover tragic pathos on the back of a dollar bill. Yet invoking Vergil, as the Great Seal does, has consequences about which it is not beside the point to be mindful. Thus, we might be made wary of how easily ignored is the fact that freedom bought or secured by force is not the freedom to which we aspire, but an imperfect parody. Acknowledging how this is so is, at least, one way to begin to do better.

19

Endgame in Sri Lanka
Dharmapala's Legacy and Rajapaksa's War

Independence from colonial rule is a people's right. But when the colonizers leave, their institutions — for instance, in government, law, education — remain and, indeed, have frequently fostered the leaders of the independence movements themselves. The oppressive legacy of colonialism might therefore continue in the government exercised by those who struggled for freedom from colonial rule in the first place. And when religion is part of the picture, things can become highly complicated. For instance, if religion is a marker of the colonized people as a group, it can be annexed to their struggle for liberation as a universal human right. But when independence is achieved, religion also might become, in turn, a means of exclusion, enabling the doing unto others what was done unto one's self.

With these points in mind, I want to look briefly at the recent violence in Sri Lanka, and at the anti-colonial struggle in the early twentieth century that helps to explain it, and in which, in turn, Buddhism played a key role.

It isn't clear how a political settlement will be reached in Sri Lanka in the wake of the recent (May 2009) overwhelming victory by government forces against the secessionist Tamil Tigers (the LTTE, Liberation Tigers of Tamil Eelam). The civil war had gone on for some twenty-six years, with at least seventy thousand people killed, and has left an incalculable legacy of suffering, trauma, and resentment that no political settlement will resolve sufficiently well.

The main architect of the recent campaign against the LTTE (recruited from Sri Lanka's minority Tamil population) is Sri Lanka's President, Mahinda Rajapaksa, elected to office in 2005. As his forces moved north, attacking Tamil Tiger strongholds in the Jaffna peninsula, civilians were caught between the two armies. The Tigers, ferocious as ever, used their own civilian population as human shields. But Rajapaksa was undeterred and continued his advance, despite international calls for a ceasefire. A current estimate is that some 7,000 people were killed in roughly a month, and some 250,000 are being held in government camps, for "processing" that might take up to two years. Aid groups and humanitarian agencies have been refused access, the press has in large part been excluded, and envoys have been cold-shouldered. As Colombo's *Daily News* curtly put it: "Get your humanitarian paws off my country" (*Globe and Mail*, 1 May 2009).

Conflict between the Sinhalese and Tamils in Sri Lanka goes back a long way. We can learn about this in the *Mahavamsa*, an ancient chronicle composed by Buddhist monks (*bhikkhus*) in the sixth century CE, and which I have briefly described in chapter 4. The *Mahavamsa* records Sri Lanka's earliest history, reaching back to legendary times. The main aim of the chronicle is to declare and celebrate the close bond between the monarchy and the *Sangha* (the community of monks, or *bhikkhus*). And so we learn about the arrival of Buddhism on the island and its subsequent protection by Sri Lanka's rulers. The *Mahavamsa* recounts the reigns of sixty-one monarchs, most of whom are treated summarily. The main exceptions are Devanampiya Tissa

(307–267 BCE) and Dutthagamini (161–137 BCE), who are praised especially for their success in unifying the people and protecting Buddhism. Here, as throughout, the *Mahavamsa* insists that Sri Lanka can be properly governed and united only by a Buddhist ruler.

Devanampiya Tissa is recorded as introducing Buddhism officially to Sri Lanka, following a visit by Mahinda, son of the Buddhist Emperor Asoka. (The Buddha himself is said to have visited Sri Lanka on three occasions during his lifetime as a special privilege to the Sinhalas, who could then think of themselves as uniquely chosen to safeguard his message.) Devanampiya Tissa subsequently established the Mahavihara, the great Buddhist monastic centre, still in existence.

But Dutthagamini is the main hero of the chronicle because of his spectacular victory over the Tamil king, Elara, who had ruled for forty-four years. We are assured that Elara was not a bad ruler, and the heroic task undertaken by Dutthagamini was not to defeat tyranny and injustice, but to restore Buddhism. When Elara is killed, Dutthagamini erects a monument in his memory, and here the *Mahavamsa* wants us to know, again, that the main aim of the war was to provide Sri Lanka with a Buddhist monarch.

And so, as Dutthagamini prepares for war he fastens a relic of the Buddha to his spear and gets help from the *Sangha*. After the battle, when he has a pang of conscience about the number of enemy dead, a delegation of monks offers comfort, assuring him that only "one and a half human beings" were actually killed. The rest were "unbelievers" and are "not more to be esteemed than beasts." The one and a half — who are explained more or less as collateral damage — were a Buddhist and a half-hearted Buddhist. Not being Buddhist, the others are not really human, and, consequently, Dutthagamini's mind can rest easy. I have cited the key passage in chapter 4, in connection with the anti-colonial *bhikkhu* Walpola Rahula.

In the early twentieth century, Dutthagamini was enthusiastically regarded as a hero by many proponents of the modern Buddhist revival and the Sinhala nationalism that went along with it as part of

Sri Lanka's (Ceylon, as it then was) struggle for independence from Britain. In the 1980s, Sri Lankan journalists could still talk about a pervasive "*Mahavamsa* mentality" in Sinhala nationalism, by which they meant a conflation of religion, ethnic identity, and the idea of a unified country ruled according to the Buddha *dharma*. As we shall see, the lesson has not been lost on the admirers of the victorious Rajapaksa, most recent conqueror of Tamil resistance and uniter of the motherland, with the blessing of the *Sangha*.

Still, the agenda driving modern Sinhala nationalism did not derive directly from the *Mahavamsa*, but was developed by way of an inventive rereading that conformed the ancient chronicle to the needs of Sri Lanka's campaign for independence, which was attained in 1948. One figure in this campaign stands out as so significant that, in the opinion of a distinguished scholarly commentator, "no major Sinhala thinker or writer after him has escaped his influence," so that he is rightly called the "founder of Buddhist modernism." This is Anagarika Dharmapala (1864–1933). His name means Homeless Protector of the Dharma, and replaces his family name, Don David Hewavitharane, because he thought the title would better indicate his vocation as a champion of Buddhism and a rebel against the colonial power.

Dharmapala was convinced that a Buddhist revival would awaken his fellow Sri Lankans from what he considered their colonial sleep-walking. He argues that Buddhism is pre-eminent among the world's religions because it transcends caste, kin, and race, while promot-ing a message of toleration and compassion. Also, he looks to the *Mahavamsa* to confirm the relationship between Buddhism and the Sinhalas, whom he describes as racially distinct, and whose histori-cal destiny is to rule Sri Lanka. Dharmapala's views about race are drawn from Western ideas current in the nineteenth century, and he insists on Sinhala racial identity in a way that the compiler of the *Mahavamsa* would not have understood.

As a schoolboy, Dharmapala had conceived a special dislike for the Bible, and got into trouble in the Christian school to which his parents had sent him as the best means of acquiring a modern education. Later, as a young man, he was inspired by the powerful Buddhist orator Mohottivatte Gunananda, whose impressive pro-Buddhist polemics against Christianity were highly influential in shaping the Buddhist revival to which Dharmapala was to commit his best energies. In turn, Gunananda recognized the young man's talent and introduced him to Colonel Henry Steel Olcott and Madame Blavatsky, founders of the Theosophical Society, who had come to Sri Lanka to organize Buddhist resistance to Christianity, especially by developing a modern Buddhist education system. Among other initiatives, Olcott produced a highly successful *Buddhist Catechism*, first published in 1881 and reissued in an expanded form in more than forty editions. Dharmapala worked assiduously for the Buddhist Theosophical Society, though eventually he fell out with Olcott and pursued his own, specifically Sri Lankan program of Buddhist revival.

Dharmapala's thinking was fundamentally shaped by these various events. From his school days he developed a poor opinion of Christianity, and especially of Christian missionaries and their colonizing countrymen. From Gunananda he learned the value of informed polemical discourse, using the enemy's oratorical techniques against them. From Olcott and Blavatsky he learned the value of a practical Buddhism that could be taught catechetically and which appealed to an urban Western-educated Sri Lankan audience. Also, Dharmapala sought to promote a modern scientific and technological education as the best way for the Sinhalas to improve their material well-being. This mix of elements was further shaped and fused by Dharmapala's own scholarly talents, irrepressible energy, and intense conviction about Sinhala national sovereignty and its sacred ties to Buddhism.

For the most part, Dharmapala's writings address specific audiences and are designed to meet the requirements of particular occasions. He was fluent in Sinhala and English, and the substantial collection of his work edited by Ananda Guruge comprises letters, addresses, journal articles, pamphlets, occasional essays, and diary entries. Yet, despite these varied contents, a small number of themes reappear constantly, often supported by the same examples and quotations. That is, Dharmapala hammers away at a core set of ideas, and once we grasp what they are, his writings hold few intellectual surprises.

Dharmapala aims first of all to promote Buddhism, which he considers superior to other religions. Thus, the Buddha is "the greatest [reformer] the world has ever seen" (351), and Dharmapala is aggressive in his denunciations of "alien faiths" (58). Especially, he condemns the monotheistic religions as "bloodthirsty, despotic, and cruel" (418). By contrast, Buddhism "admits the perfect equality of all men, it proclaims the universal brotherhood" (21) and insists on compassion and toleration.

Dharmapala then adds that Buddhism is fundamentally in tune with the empirical views and attitudes of Western science. Repeatedly, he claims science as the ally of Buddhism and the enemy of Christianity. "Buddhism is a scientific religion" (20) which regards the world as developing by way of an "unerring natural Immutable Law of Cause and Effect" (79) rather than "by the will of a foolish ignorant despotic phantom creator" (79). The conviction that Buddhism is a "pure science" (658) enables Dharmapala to berate the current generation of *bhikkhus* (519) as ill-educated — like far too many Sinhalas, they are "indolent, ignorant, illiterate" (721). Dharmapala blames this sad state of affairs on colonialism, which prevented scientific and technological advances among the native people, all the better to enable the colonial "freebooters" to do what they always do, namely "to plunder and destroy ancient civilizations" (398). Instead of offering an education based on technology and industry, the colonizers used their schools mostly to promote Christianity. For this reason, Dharmapala exhorts young Sinhalas to go abroad "to learn technical sciences" and then return to work for their country. By such means the Sinhalas can awaken from the "alien rule" which merely "stupefies" them, while also recovering the true spirit of Buddhism.

In describing the pure Buddhism from which the modern Sinhalas have so tragically departed, Dharmapala looks especially to the *Mahavamsa*. He is captivated by the idea that the chronicle records a time when there was "a purely religious civilization" (486) throughout the island. Dharmapala waxes lyrical about the glories of the ancient kingdom, inviting us to imagine the "pure, refined, kind-hearted children of Lanka" (482). "A more joyous, contented race, it is impossible to imagine" (384) than these people who "were free from pride, envy, crime and luxury" (514) and among whom "there was no jealousy and hatred" (295). But the colonizers corrupted these perfect, beautiful Buddhist children of Lanka, who then fell into indolence, superstition, and servility. And so Dharmapala looks forward to a revival that will restore the island to its original glory, both Buddhist and Sinhala. "Lanka, the pearl of the Indian Ocean, the resplendent jewel" is once more to be the "repository of the pure religion of the Tathagato [Buddha]" (481).

To confirm his conviction about the singularity of the Sinhalas, Dharmapala supplements his reading of the *Mahavamsa* with late-nineteenth-century Western theories about racial identity. He refers repeatedly to the Sinhalas as "Aryan" and assures us that they are "a unique race" (479), "a superior race" (515), but through the fault of the colonizers "the Aryan Sinhalese has lost his true identity and become a hybrid" (494). Even the simplest Sinhala peasant has religion "in his blood" (540), and "to the historian of the Aryan race a knowledge of the five Nikayas [Buddhist scriptures] is essential" (499). And so the compact between ethnicity, nationalism, and religion is copper-fastened, as Dharmapala mobilizes his countrymen to recover the lost ancestral utopia — a united Buddhist Sri Lanka where people will live once more without "pride, envy, crime, and luxury" (524).

The trouble with utopias is that they can't be realized, but if you are convinced that innate racial superiority and special divine appointment declare otherwise in your case, then, inevitably, you will scapegoat some other group. Despite his commendable anti-colonialism, Dharmapala does just this when he looks yet again to the *Mahavamsa,* and, not surprisingly, he turns to the exploits of Dutthagamini.

Dharmapala begins by characterizing the Tamils as "fiercely antagonistic to Buddhism," but the "wonderful prince" Dutthagamini intervened to ensure "the re-establishment of the religion of the supreme Buddha." The subsequent war was of a truly "religious character" and was, we are assured, "conducted in a spirit of religion." Throughout the Dutthagamini story, Buddhism is "completely identified with the racial individuality of the people" (488–89). Dutthagamini is "our heroic and patriot king" (501), and Dharmapala exhorts an audience of young Sinhala men likewise to "enter into the realms of our King Dutugamunu in spirit and try to identify yourself with the thoughts of that great king who rescued Buddhism and our nationalism from oblivion" (510). The young men are invited to affirm the inseparability of race, religion, and nationalism and also to accept that violence might be required to preserve an integral Sinhala Buddhist Sri Lanka.

For Dharmapala, colonialism is the chief enemy. But when independence was achieved in 1948, the colonizers left and Sri Lanka entered into a post-colonial phase, at first promising but then increasingly troubled. One problem was that the ancient enemy, the Tamils, were seen as having been favoured in education and employment by the British, and consequently they replaced the colonizers as a chief impediment to the realization of Dharmapala's utopian dream. And so the ancient antagonism resurfaced with atrocious violence on both sides, until Mahinda Rajapaksa, our modern Dutthagamini, put his armies into the field.

The recent, appalling war needs to be understood against this background of a modern Buddhist revival spearheaded by Dharmapala. This is so not least because Rajapaksa often represents and reproduces the main elements of Dharmapala's agenda, though he is less explicitly racist and less willing to mock and vilify religions other than Buddhism. Nonetheless, he stands firmly in the Dharmapala tradition, and he hangs on to the old Sinhala Buddhist exceptionalism. This becomes clear in his virtual deification by his Sinhala supporters, among whom the old prejudices remain vigorous, however much concealed, officially, from the world's full view.

For instance, in his presidential address (4 February 2009) to mark the sixty-first anniversary of independence, Rajapaksa begins by praising the "struggle" that led to Sri Lanka being "freed from the clutches of British Imperialism." Colonialism prevented "the progress of our nation," and especially the acquisition of modern technology. The potential for such progress is "inherent in our nature," and just as the colonizers blocked the "proper path of unity and progress," so, today, "scapegoat, racist and terrorist politics" are again seeking to divide us. Rajapaksa then recalls the "bravery, national pride and patriotism" of the ancient kings, first among whom is "Dutugemunu." Today, our forces revive the "great heroism and dignity of the past" to ensure "the unitary nature" of Sri Lanka. Rajapaksa goes on to advise his countrymen that "the remnants and leftovers of subjugation should be erased from our minds," because our "future as a people" is glorious as we move towards a "national reawakening" marked by "pride and dignity." He ends by extending the traditional Buddhist "Blessing of the Noble Triple Gem."

The speech rings all the main Dharmapala keynotes. Colonial repression (now replaced by "racist" terrorism) prevents technological progress and the unification of Sri Lanka that will ensure a glorious future. Sri Lankans must recover their dignity and be resolute and heroic like Dutthagamini, and the speech ends with a Buddhist blessing. Significantly, Rajapaksa doesn't mention the Tamils by name, or, for that matter, the Sinhalas, and in a neat pre-emptive move he accuses the terrorists of racism — a charge which he well knows has been directed against the Sinhalas. In a victory day speech (3 June 2009) he fills out the picture.

Again, Rajapaksa anticipates "the dawn of a great and distinguished future" and then adds some lines in Tamil, saying that the war was not fought "against the Tamil people" but against the LTTE, and now the war "against the terrorists is over." After this conciliatory paragraph, Rajapaksa goes on to praise his armed forces at some length. He concludes by noticing that Sri Lanka has fought off "ruthless invaders" for thousands of years, and again invokes "King Dutugemunu." The lessons of these great battles of the past, he says, "are impressed on our flesh, blood and bones," as our brave soldiers have shown. He blames the terrorists for using "innocent Tamil people" as human shields and claims that his own troops acted honourably and with restraint, showing "kindness and compassion." In the new Sri Lanka, there "will not even be an iota of space for racism and separatism" and education will pave the way for technological progress. Sri Lanka will be ruled under "our Lion Flag," and the blessing of the Noble Triple Gem is again extended.

Rajapaksa is careful to distinguish between the separatist and racist "terrorists" and the Tamil population in general, but in invoking Dutthagamini and stating that the ancient Sinhala victories are "ingrained in our flesh, blood and bones," he falls back into a familiar, more disturbing pattern of thinking, less reassuring than the well-practised gestures towards kindness and compassion. And the "Lion Flag" under which Sri Lanka is now united bears the Sinhala emblem, the lion, *sinha*. Elsewhere, Rajapaksa states clearly that "the doctrine of the Lord Buddha demonstrates the correct path to life. Accordingly we have given the teachings of the Lord Buddha the utmost place in our governance system as it paves the way for a new Sri Lanka."

The Dharmapala agenda has not been lost on Rajapaksa, and his enthralled supporters make this aspect of the victorious campaign embarrassingly clear. Doug Saunders reports from Colombo that large statues, billboards, and posters "on every street corner, every public building, every shop front," announce that Rajapaksa "has saved the nation and deserves to be crowned king." Rajapaksa is shown dressed in the white robes of a Buddhist deity, and Saunders cites a typical opinion, voiced by a twenty-year-old student, praising Rajapaksa as a leader "who has made our island into one kingdom." And then, "Why do we need elections any more? He is the king we need." Sanjana Hattotuwa, a democracy activist at the Centre for Policy Alternatives in Colombo, is cited by Saunders as ruefully noticing that the popular response has been "singularly Buddhist in nature and expression," portraying Rajapaksa as a king along the lines of the old monarchs praised "in the Mahawansa" (*Globe and Mail*, 26 May 2009). For their part, the monastic council of the Mahavihara awarded Rajapaksa its highest honour for his services in uniting the country (*ColomboPage*, 18 June 2009). In turn, Rajapaksa assured the monks that he would make Sri Lanka "an island of dharma once again without delay," shaping it on the model of the ancient kings (*ColomboPage*, 20 June 2009).

Not surprisingly, comparisons with Dutthagamini abound. As we see, Rajapaksa himself evokes the ancient warrior king, but the analogy comes at us from many directions. C.P. Kuruppu explains that "for most Sinhalese, President Mahinda Rajapaksa is the modern version of King Dutugemunu," and "Mahinda's image of a modern Dutugemunu has given his party a clear mandate" (*The Week*, 28 June 2009). Remarkably, the Ministry of Defense issued a statement by H.L.D. Mahindapala, praising Rajapaksa for having "repeated all over again the history of Dutugemunu" (23 June 2009). The article goes on to ask who is the greater leader, and concludes, well, yes, Rajapaksa is "the one who outshines Dutugemunu." A popular music video (one of many) praises "the great king" who "performed a miracle to unify our country," and the lyricist, Sunil R. Gamage, claims to have used the word "miracle" because it is normally associated with the Buddha. A well-known filmmaker, Jayantha Chandrasiri, is making a film about Dutthagamini and received personal congratulations from Rajapaksa himself (*ColomboPage*, 3 June 2009).

Apparently, the *"Mahavamsa* mentality" remains alive and well, and Rajapaksa's triumph needs to be seen, in part, as a further episode of Dharmapala's Buddhist revival, with its nationalist, ethnocentric agenda. Today's political leaders in Sri Lanka do not stress the connection to Dharmapala, whose racist theories and explicit religious bigotry are not acceptable currency, especially on the international stage, his admirable anti-colonialism notwithstanding. But although many international observers of Sri Lanka might not know much about Dharmapala, the Sinhalas themselves, by and large, know a good deal. What is going on in the streets tells us this all too clearly, and in Rajapaksa's promised "island of dharma," the exceptionalist, ancestral utopia still exerts its fatal attraction. The ideal of a free people in a perfect Sri Lanka — such as described by Dharmapala — is itself a commendable goal. But insofar as the actual imperfections of Sri Lanka are projected onto others who happen, for instance, not to be Buddhist, the ideal itself becomes a carrier of the poison to which it should be the antidote.

20

Jung and The Secret of the Golden Flower

In chapter 16, on *Romeo and Juliet,* I noticed briefly that human sexuality is partly driven by the unconscious, and, consequently, we are less free in our love-choices (as in much else) than we might think. By insisting that decision making is not altogether rational but an expression also of drives, fixations, and compulsions of which we are unaware, Sigmund Freud revolutionized the understanding of free choice and moral responsibility.

In the following pages I want to focus on Carl Gustav Jung (1875–1961), who was Freud's most important follower, despite the eventual quarrel and separation between them. Jung had a special interest in Eastern religions, and in his commentary on the Taoist-Buddhist *The Secret of the Golden Flower,* he explores the main themes with which I am concerned in this book as a whole: the relationships, that is, between imperfection, the self, and freedom.

Jung first met Freud in Vienna in 1907 and remained closely associated with him for the next six years. When the relationship ended in disagreement, Jung entered into a period of lonely, intense introspection. During this time — roughly, from 1913 to 1919 — his own distinctive insights and theories took shape.

Freud had looked mainly to early childhood experience as a source of his patients' neuroses, which he linked also to sexuality. Jung preferred to locate the neurosis in the present and to consider sexuality as one expression of a broader vital energy, which he called *libido*. Also, for Jung, the psyche is a self-regulating system, and neurosis is an attempt to restore equilibrium, thereby correcting habitual, one-sided patterns of behaviour which are distortive and cause illness. In turn, self-regulation entails an interplay of opposing libidinal energies, and the bulk of Jung's work is devoted to charting and describing what he saw as the main patterns of opposition, the dynamic processes through which personality develops — or is achieved, as he liked to say.

Jung's practice as a medical doctor allowed him access to mentally ill patients, and his extraordinary learning in mythology, philosophy, and the history of ideas enabled him to link the findings of his clinical practice to the world's great religions and systems of mythology. In so doing, he was surprised to discover how the delusions, dreams, and fantasies of patients could reproduce mythological and traditional symbolic motifs of which the patients had no prior knowledge. Jung undertook to explain this interesting discovery by suggesting that there is an analogy between the evolution of the unconscious and the evolution of the body. That is, because of our evolution as a species, human bodies are basically similar despite the variety of actual human beings. So also, the unconscious is the result of an evolutionary development whereby patterns of behaviour are set down, so that the mind's unconscious operations are similarly structured, despite the variety of individual manifestations. Jung named these basic patterns "archetypes," by which he meant organizational tendencies that give rise to specific kinds of images and symbols, both in the dreams and delusions of patients and also in the productions of culture, such as art, religion, and mythology.

For Jung, archetypes declare themselves especially in symbols, which are a bridge to the unconscious but which merely represent and do not encompass the underlying energies upon which consciousness floats like a bubble on the ocean. In the case of an ill patient, the spontaneous symbols in dreams or hallucinations can be messages indicating the kinds of rebalancing, or adaptation, necessary to restore the free flow of energy in which health consists. In a broader cultural context, the symbolism and imagery of religion, mythology, art, and literature perform a similar function, helping to maintain a healthy equilibrium between consciousness and the unconscious — the busy waking world and the tacit dimensions of the dark powers that sustain it. "All religions are therapies for the sorrows and disorders of the soul," Jung says (*The Secret of the Golden Flower,* 127). Likewise, psychoanalysis is "a highly moral task of immense educational value" (*The Essential Jung,* 54). This conviction that religion is therapeutic and that psychoanalysis is educational blurs the distinction between patients and ordinary people. Consequently, for Jung, the task of balancing the energies that contend within ourselves is shared by everyone, and we are never entirely free of it, though some make the necessary adaptations more efficiently than others.

By reflecting on such issues, Jung developed a distinctive system and set of terms outlining, as it were, the anatomy of the unconscious. Popular summaries of his thought tell us about the shadow (the dark side of each of us), persona (how we present ourselves to the world), anima and animus (the female dimension of the male unconscious and vice versa), the old wise man (spiritual wisdom), and self (Jung used this term in a special sense, to indicate the integrated or balanced personality, embracing consciousness and the unconscious, and encompassing the ego). Together with the basic distinction between two main types of personality (which he named extravert and introvert), and the four main functions (thinking, feeling, sensation, intuition), these ideas are the backbone of Jung's thinking insofar as we might describe it as a system. But Jung formulated his ideas gradually, shaping them out of his clinical experience and relentless study, and his voluminous writings record not only the evolution of his main theories but also his own quest for a well-integrated self — the wholeness of personality which he thought the most important human achievement and which he described as "individuation."

Jung thought that only a minority of exceptional individuals are able to strike out on their own path, defying convention in order to achieve authentic personal development. Most of us make do with habitual and conventional ways of knowing and behaving, which provide sufficient security to enable us to manage life's crises more or less adequately. "The vast majority of mankind do not choose their own way, but convention, and consequently develop not themselves but a method and a collective mode of life at the cost of their own wholeness" (*The Essential Jung*, 198). By contrast, the "only meaningful life" is the one that "strives for the individual realization — absolute and unconditional — of its own particular law" (204–5), and this is what Jung means by freedom. Consequently, each of us struggles alone on an individual path, and because this is so, Jung insists that he uses no particular therapeutic method in treating a patient: "I let pure experience decide the therapeutic aims" (210); "Each of us carries his own life-form within him — an irrational form which no others can outbid" (211). Elsewhere, he says that progress "cannot be indicated in the form of a recipe" (226), and, again, there "can be no self-knowledge based on theoretical assumptions" (352).

Nonetheless, Jung also claims that freedom of self-determination is limited. The unconscious "irrational life-process" in which we are all immersed exerts a powerful influence on behaviour, but it also "expresses itself in definite symbols," and, for the analyst, "knowledge of the symbols is indispensable" (226). That is, it is helpful to know how to read the language of symbols, even though conscious understanding cannot (by definition) encompass the unconscious with which symbolism puts us in touch. Consequently, for Jung the path to freedom, personal growth, and wisdom is dialectical, entailing a reconciliation of opposite energies, chief among which is the polarization of consciousness and the unconscious. The same dialectical process is evident in every aspect of our psychic life: "There is no balance, no system of self-regulation, without opposition. The psyche is just such a self-regulating system" (167). Elsewhere he says, "the self is a union of opposites *par excellence*"; it is "absolutely paradoxical in that it represents in every respect thesis and antithesis, and at the same time synthesis" (269). Jung never tired of repeating this idea, and of seeking the means of finding a still point of tension between the opposites — the dynamic equilibrium in which fullness of life is realized.

Still, despite his theoretical statements about the perfect wholeness of an integrated personality, Jung insists that the process of integration is in fact never complete. "Personality, as the complete realization of our whole being, is an unattainable ideal. But unattainability is no argument against the ideal, for ideals are only signposts, never the goal" (196). This remarkable statement (and there are others like it) confirms the imperfection of our actual experience while acknowledging the fact that we can't know about imperfection without being conscious also of the ideal. All of which brings us back to the tension within Jung's writing between his individual struggle for understanding (his particular path) and the idealizing aspects of his "system." That is, Jung's writings are partly his own self-exploration, and he presents us with something of a personal mythology, despite his claims for scientific objectivity. It can be difficult — frustrating and intriguing by turns — to distinguish between these aspects of his work, and this difficulty is especially evident in Jung's commentary on the eighteenth-century Chinese Taoist-Buddhist text, *The Secret of the Golden Flower.*

Jung tells us that Richard Wilhelm (a missionary to China and a scholar of Chinese language and culture) sent him a copy of *The Secret of the Golden Flower* in 1928, and Jung wrote a commentary which was published along with Wilhelm's translation in 1929. Jung had already discussed Taoism in some detail in *Psychological Types* (1918), but he singles out *The Secret of the Golden Flower* as nonetheless "critical for my own work" because it helped him especially to understand the "processes of the collective unconscious" (xiii) with which he had struggled in the years after his break with Freud in 1913. Jung explains how *The Secret of the Golden Flower* enabled him to understand the symbolic language of alchemy, which in turn provided him with valuable information on the structure and dynamics of the psyche. Also, through Taoism, Jung came to understand the self as constituted by a balance between consciousness and the unconscious. "The aim of Taoist ethics," Jung says in *Psychological Types,* "is to find deliverance from the cosmic tension of opposites by a return to *tao*" (*CW* 6, para. 370), and in *The Secret of the Golden Flower* he describes how he found a new way to explore "the unity of life and consciousness" (103) through the idea of the self. He also arrived at a new understanding of how symbols mediate between consciousness and the unconscious, and in this context he sets out for the first time in detail his ideas about the therapeutic agency of what he called "active imagination."

Still, as scholars keep pointing out, there is a lot wrong with Jung's understanding of *The Secret of the Golden Flower* and what he often sweepingly refers to as the "East." Briefly, as a direct result of his conviction that the psyche is a self-regulating system, Jung convinced himself that Western rationalism is one-sided and prone to ego-inflation. The West therefore needs the "more profound" (*CW* 13, para. 2) wisdom of the East, which Jung thought was less rational and more in tune with the unconscious. The idea of a counterbalance to excessive rationality is fair enough, but, astonishingly, Jung proposes that, for instance, an Indian, "inasmuch as he is really Indian, does not think" (*CW* 10, para. 1007); also, in terms of intellectual development, the East (to which Jung denied any genuine philosophical tradition) is "childish" (*CW* 13, para. 8) compared to the West.

The extravagance of such generalizations, impatient of the diversity of cultures which he lumps, simply, under "East" and "West," is now broadly recognized. So also is the exaggeration of Jung's warnings to Westerners not to get too close to Eastern teachings for fear of doing themselves grave psychological damage. Since Jung's day, cultural cross-currents consequent upon rapid globalization have especially made his overconfident binaries seem arrogant and silly, as they are.

Added to these problems is the fact that Wilhelm's translation of *The Secret of the Golden Flower* is often misleading or faulty, and the text with which he worked is incomplete and otherwise imperfect. In short, although Wilhelm and Jung were pioneers in making *The Secret of the Golden Flower* available in Europe, Wilhelm's shortcomings are, by modern standards, considerable, and for his part, Jung tends to reshape the (already imperfect) text uncritically in the image of his own special understanding of the psyche.

Still, the Wilhelm-Jung version of *The Secret of the Golden Flower* remains interesting, for two main reasons. First, Jung does have an appreciative understanding of the main ideas of Taoism, and he responds warmly to the basic Taoist teaching that complementary but opposite energies might be aligned in a skilfully lived life in harmony with the *Tao,* which is both the way and the goal — the mystery of origins beyond reason, by which we are both sustained and constituted. Second, Jung's encounter with *The Secret of the Golden Flower* showed him that in his own psychoanalytic practice he had been "unconsciously led along that secret way which has been the preoccupation of the best minds of the East for centuries" (86). Consequently, *The Secret of the Golden Flower* is a linchpin in Jung's own development, helping him to understand the collective unconscious, the process of integration towards a balanced self, and the significance of images and symbols in effecting this process.

Throughout the *commentary,* these two strands — the scholarly assessment of Taoism and the development of Jung's own thinking — are interwoven. In attempting to unravel them, it is better, on the one hand, not to discount Jung's understanding of Taoism or, on the other, to read the *commentary* solely as another chapter in the narrative of Jung's personal development. And so we return to the contrast between Jung's ideas, for which he claimed objective validity, and the individuality of the path he explored, resistant to imitation by others.

Rather than dwell further on the task of unravelling these strands, I would like to focus briefly on how the *commentary* highlights its own resistance to the systematic dimensions of Jung's thinking to which it also gives expression. This aspect of the *commentary* is not usually noticed, but the dialectical process by which the mystery of personality opens upon the mystery of the unconscious remains, for Jung, open-ended, and in the *commentary* he invites us to see how this is so.

For instance, Jung insists that the journey each of us takes through life is irreducibly individual, even though the goal can be described in universal terms. Consequently, "the method is merely the path, the direction taken by a man" (83), and the way forward "must not be pigeonholed under any heading, for then it becomes a recipe to be applied mechanically" (92). Rather, we are perpetually taken up in "the paradoxes and the polarity inherent in what is alive" (85), and we need to recognize that the "ideal can be completely realized only in death," which alone frees us from illusions. "Until then there are real and relatively real figures of the unconscious" (115); meanwhile, we seek as well as we can for fullness of life, recognizing and acknowledging the unconscious "as far as possible" (124). By such means we might best mitigate suffering and learn to live with a kind of conscious detachment (124) from the shocks and misfortunes of the world. In the end, after death, "what happens to the detached consciousness" (125) is not for a psychologist to say. Indeed, "Every statement about the transcendental is to be avoided because it is invariably only a laughable presumption on the part of the human mind." Although the terms "God" or "Tao" can be used to say something about the "knowable," these terms say "nothing about the unknowable, about which nothing can be determined" (135).

Admittedly, Jung can be tendentious and exasperating, but there is also something compellingly thoughtful in his explanation of relationships between the conscious mind and the oceanic unconscious from which it emerges. As we see, his thinking evolves towards a central set of ideas and concepts, but his powerful, gifted mind was also on its own quest, which, as Jung well knew, his theories could not adequately describe or encompass. And so he wondered at the mystery of things, the sheer strangeness of the world and of our alarming consciousness within it, perilously suspended in a cosmos of incomprehensible dimensions and emergent from an equally unfathomable unconscious. He understood the limits of what we can know — for instance, what happens after we die, or how understanding emerges from the deepest recesses of our bodies. For him, the task in hand remains the way itself, the Tao, which he thought each person should follow affirmatively and with courage. And so Jung remained open to the overarching mystery, but he was keen also to avoid the "laughable presumption" that we can know it other than by dwelling within the dialectical process by which it declares itself. In and through this process we might find transcendent moments of beauty, joy, understanding, and freedom, yet without fully realizing the ideal wholeness, which remains nonetheless to infuse and sustain our aspirations.

Kieslowski's Red
Fraternity in the Making

Krzysztof Kieslowski's (1941–96) best-known films are his *Three Colours* trilogy, comprising *Blue* (liberty), *White* (equality), and *Red* (fraternity). Given that the main topic of this section is freedom, *Blue* seems the obvious candidate for discussion. But I want to comment on *Red*, because, as the trilogy itself indicates, liberty and equality are incompletely realized until they are fulfilled in fraternity. Just as *Red* is the summation of Kieslowski's vision, so the way in which freedom opens upon fraternity is the summation also of what I want to say both in this section and in the book as a whole.

In other ways, *Red* also supports the main suggestions I have been making throughout this book about the self, imperfection, and freedom, and how these topics invite religious answers. Kieslowski is skeptical about religion, but he understands how the strangeness and mystery of consciousness, of our personal interactions, and of existence itself can awaken a religious sensibility or, at least, a meta-physical curiosity informed by a sense of wonder. He is fascinated by chance, coincidence, and by the limited freedoms of imperfect human beings whose identities are frequently unstable or provisional, finding their way towards moral understanding and compassion. At best, his characters achieve a fragile but tenacious fraternity, the kind of mutual appreciation and exchange upon which the social fabric depends and by means of which it might remake itself, in the teeth, if necessary, of prevailing ideological prescriptions. But before getting to *Red*, I will say a little about Kieslowski's career as a whole.

The Kieslowski Project

Krzysztof Kieslowski began his career as a documentary filmmaker in his native Poland. In a series of films during the 1960s and 1970s, he focused on people's everyday lives. In so doing, he revealed some uncomfortable differences between the idealizing propaganda of the communist regime in Poland and people's actual experience. But as with all films made in Poland at the time, Kieslowski's had to be approved by a censorship board, and several were shelved. As he explains, a code soon developed between audiences and filmmakers by means of which criticisms of the government were offered obliquely, through verbal and visual subtleties that the censors failed to identify. "The public faultlessly recognized our intentions," Kieslowski says, "so we communicated over the censors' heads" (152).

In the years preceding the Solidarity trade union movement in Poland during the 1980s, filmmakers did much to awaken and stimulate public criticism of the government: "We were together, us and the public, in the aversion we had for a system we didn't accept." Kieslowski regrets that "today this basic reason for being together doesn't exist any more" (152), but he never surrendered the lessons he learned in making those early documentaries. His (notoriously) precise attention to everyday objects and his reliance on audiences to read nuances and unobtrusive patterns of significance remain basic to his feature films, even though these films do not deal overtly with political themes. Ironically, when Kieslowski moved to France in the late 1980s, he found that economic censorship (based on catering to what is thought to be public taste) was more restrictive than censorship under the communists (152). Still, he refused to make box-office success a main concern; nonetheless, his late features were critically acclaimed and widely viewed by appreciative audiences.

Kieslowski explains that he moved away from documentaries because their intrusiveness upon people's private lives made him uncomfortable. "I'm frightened of those real tears. In fact, I don't know whether I've got the right to photograph them. At such times I feel like somebody who's found himself in a realm which is, in fact, out of bounds. That's the main reason why I escaped from documentaries" (86). And so, between 1979 and 1988, Kieslowski made nine films, six of which were features. Also, he made the *Decalogue* (1988), a ten-part TV drama series based on the Ten Commandments. The *Decalogue* brought Kieslowski international attention, and subsequently he moved to France, where he made *The Double Life of Véronique* (1991) and *Three Colours* (*Blue, White, Red*) (1993–94), which established his reputation.

Despite the fact that his documentaries had political implications, Kieslowski was never comfortable in the political arena. He recounts two small-scale ventures into politics, both of which were disastrous. "I had a painful feeling of having walked into a room where I absolutely shouldn't have gone," and he realized, "it wasn't my world" (39). That is, temperamentally he wasn't cut out for politics, and the mildly cantankerous, wryly pessimistic, anti-authoritarian, sensitive, winningly self-deprecating, and highly distinctive personality that emerges from the extended interviews with Danusia Stok confirms the point. Even a brief look at Kieslowski's account of the comic blundering by which he, as a nineteen-year-old, contrived (successfully) to avoid conscription shows that whatever gifts in the making we might detect in the young Kieslowski, they are hardly likely to be the sort that would produce a public figure.

But there is a further significant dimension to Kieslowski's disengagement from politics, which he explains in his reaction to the imposition of martial law in Poland in 1981. "I realized that politics aren't really important," he says, because politics "don't solve the important human questions" (144). Whether you live in a communist or a capitalist country, certain "essential, fundamental" questions remain, "questions like, What is the meaning of life? Why get up in the morning? Politics don't answer that" (144). Kieslowski goes on to explain that even when his films were "about people involved in politics," he was trying, mainly, "to find out what sort of people they were. The political environment only formed a background. Even the short documentary films were always about people, about what they're like. They weren't political films. Politics were never the subject" (144).

The documentaries, then, are political because for Kieslowski they are first of all personal. That is, in recording the lives of ordinary people, Kieslowski implicitly criticized official depictions of how things were in communist Poland. Still, he explains that even "the fanatical advocates of Communism in the 1950s" weren't pursuing evil ends; rather, they aspired to do good, and there is no shame or disgrace in that (124). Their actions were "simply a mistake," and we need to understand "that this theory is impossible to realize in practice and that it has to lead to evil being done" (124). For Kieslowski, that is always the problem when ideals or principles are too vigorously pursued. The fact is, people's everyday lives show that too much remains unaccounted for by the generalizations of the moralists and ideologues. Personal experience is too complex, too bound up in the perplexities and irreducible conundrums of our imperfect human condition to be shaped and formed in the exact likeness of a perfect ideal. The young Kieslowski's aversion to uniforms was, basically, an aversion to uniformity, and he is unfailingly discerning about our imperfect understanding of how ethical principles apply — or fail to apply — to ourselves. "One would like to be ultimately honest, but one can't. With all the decisions you make every day, you can never be ultimately honest." Rather, he is aware of "something like a barometer" within himself, indicating what limits he should observe, and although this barometer doesn't prevent him from making wrong decisions, it gives him bearings. Still, this process "has nothing to do with any description or exact definition of right and wrong. It has to do with concrete, everyday decisions" (149). We are "tiny and imperfect," and we are unfree even though we struggle for freedom. "I'm somebody who doesn't know, somebody who's searching" (194), Kieslowski says, and he distrusts people "who show you the way, who know" (36), and who prescribe accordingly.

By contrast, Kieslowski explains that his feature films attempt "to capture what lies within us," even though "there's no way of filming it. You can only get nearer to it" (174). In his attempts to "get nearer," Kieslowski draws especially on his skills as a documentary filmmaker, which remain evident in the precise recording of everyday details and also in a characteristic absence of dramatic action. "I don't know how to narrate action," Kieslowski admits, and, as with the documentaries, "my feature films unfold more with the help of an idea rather than the help of an action" (102).

But what are we to make of this reference to "an idea," given Kieslowski's resistance to prescriptive generalization? Perhaps the word "theme" better describes what actually goes on in his features — as, for instance, in *Three Colours* he explores liberty (*Blue*), equality (*White*), and fraternity (*Red*). These are the colours of the French flag, associated with the three-word shibboleth of the French Revolution. All of which might seem all too obviously political, except that the films deal with particular personal crises in the lives of the characters, by means of which Kieslowski explores the complexities and ambiguities of what liberty, equality, and fraternity might mean: "How do the three words liberty, equality and fraternity function today? — on a very human, intimate and personal plane and not a philosophical let alone a political or social one" (212). The intimate feeling-states, subtleties of communication, intuitions, imperfections, fragilities, protective biases, courage, generosity, uncertainty (and excessive certainty) that mark our everyday experience in a world of which we have limited understanding, encompassed by the impenetrable strangeness of existence, death, chance, time, and freedom are the lifeblood of Kieslowski's films. His special magic emerges from a tension (a favourite word of his) between the material complexities of our condition and the metaphysical dimensions of time, chance, and coincidence in which we also find ourselves inexplicably immersed. Yet Kieslowski never looks to theology or religion for answers to the metaphysical questions he poses; rather, he allows us a sense of the mystery of existence itself, from which religion takes its own, different life. He knew there is too much that we don't know, and a reductive materialism or escapist supernaturalism alike betray our necessary ambivalence and uncertainty.

Kieslowski once said that he doesn't trust movies, only audiences, and he wants his films to be the equivalent of sitting down and having a chat. Yet he also knew that his films would appeal to people whose sensibilities are attuned to the subtleties of feeling, intuition, and tacit communication that he investigates. "Either you feel it or you don't" (216), he says, commenting on *Three Colours,* and he admits that *The Double Life of Véronique* is "a film for a very limited group of people. I don't mean an age group or a social group but a group of people who are sensitive to the sort of emotions shown in the film" (189). He goes on to insist that such people can come from all conditions in life and are not an elite, "unless we call sensitive people élite" (189). An analogy might be to lyric poetry. People who read lyric poetry often and with pleasure are a minority among readers. They might come from all walks of life, and as a group they are distinctive only because they have a sensibility attuned to the subtleties and revelatory power of that special means of communication. Just so, Kieslowski is a lyric poet among filmmakers. "Yes, absolutely" Kieslowski is a poet, says Jean-Louis Trintignant, reflecting on his experience in *Red,* where Trintignant and Irène Jacob played the leading roles. And so it might be helpful to consider briefly Kieslowski's own view of the creative process, and the kind of appeal his particular kind of filmic poetry has.

As we have seen, Kieslowski points to "something like a barometer" within himself when he makes moral choices which, typically, he experiences as more complex than is allowed by a plain "description of right and wrong." In the same context he refers to an "inner compass," a term he applies both to moral choices and to filmmaking. He explains that he doesn't film things "in a certain way" so that critics "will understand what it's supposed to mean" (191). Rather, the process "comes naturally to me," and "if you haven't got your own compass within yourself which clearly points you in a certain direction then you won't find it" (191). Elsewhere he says that "I don't know how ideas come to me," and repeats that he doesn't "analyze" or "rationalize." His ideas "come of their own accord," arising not from a single principle or source, but "from everything you've touched" (105). That is, the creative process expresses an entire sensibility and has its own highly personal integrity ("authenticity" [105], Kieslowski says) about which one ought not to be overly self-conscious, especially during the creative process itself.

In all this, Kieslowski describes what John Keats means by "negative capability." That is, the poet, like other kinds of artist, feels or senses the power of an image or metaphor without analyzing its implications. Analysis after the fact might provide understanding (more or less), but creative power emerges from a distinctive quality of imagination, an ability to sense, feel, intuit, and shape the image, which might well contain a great deal more than the artist realizes at the time.

Kieslowski's insistence that he doesn't analyze leads him to some statements that might at first seem to be disavowals of imagination, rather than the reverse. "I don't film metaphors" (193), he says, and, shortly after: "When I film a scene with a bottle of milk," the bottle "is simply a bottle of milk; when it spills, it means milk's been spilt. Nothing more." Yet Kieslowski quickly adds an important qualification. Other people might read certain images and scenes as metaphors, and Kieslowski says this "is very good." Although for him the spilt milk is just that, it might also turn out, after the fact, "to mean something else," which, Kieslowski says, is "a miracle"— the kind of thing achieved only by great films. Consequently, the filming itself has to be literal, but, paradoxically, "if I have a goal, then it is to escape from this literalism" (195).

The apparent contradiction here is resolved when we see Kieslowski's "inner compass" as indicating how he senses or feels the weight and affective power of an image, without too much interference by way of analysis. If milk is spilled at a certain point, the filmmaker feels that it is somehow significant, even though (following the principle of negative capability) he does not think too much about it during the creative process itself. Afterwards, the further significance of the image might emerge in a way that can, as Kieslowski says, "transport" an audience, and this is the "miracle" of art.

Kieslowski is not theoretically sophisticated when he talks about such things; rather, he sticks close to his own practice. Filming the bottle of milk and insisting that it is, primarily, just that, is what the documentary filmmaker does. But the "inner compass" of imagination also guides him, and Kieslowski's special genius lies in how the closely observed, concrete particulars can reveal people's inner lives and provoke us to consider and wonder at the mysterious dimensions of ordinary experience, including the tangle of our involvements with one another. The documentary filmmaker who recorded the revealing particulars of people's daily lives with a subtlety that the censors couldn't detect (though audiences could) puts the same unobtrusive tact to work in his features.

Let us now turn to *Red,* Kieslowski's favourite among his films and the one he considered the summation of his work. He announced his retirement when he had completed it in 1994. Shortly afterwards, in 1996, he died during heart surgery, in Warsaw.

Red

A summary of the main action of *Red* is fairly straightforward. Valentine is a student and part-time model in Geneva. She is in an unsatisfactory relationship with her boyfriend, Michel, who telephones to enquire, jealously, about her day-to-day activities. Valentine also has a younger brother, Marc, who is a drug addict, about whom she worries. Michel and Marc do not appear in the film, but we overhear their telephone conversations with Valentine in her apartment, which is located above a café, *Chez Joseph*.

Valentine's neighbour across the street is Auguste. He lives in an apartment, with his dog, and is a law student about to sit his final exams. Auguste is in a relationship with Karin, who runs a phone-in weather report business. Valentine and Auguste do not know one another, but are repeatedly filmed in the same frame, so that the (omniscient) camera suggests that they somehow belong together.

While driving through an intersection (where a giant billboard will by and by display her in her role as a professional model), Valentine runs over a dog. She brings the dog, Rita, to its owner, an elderly, retired judge, Joseph Kern, who lives in a comfortable but unkempt villa. The judge is embittered and cynical, and is indifferent to the injured animal. Valentine then drives to a vet, who discovers that Rita will soon have pups. Later, while Valentine is exercising her, the now recovered Rita runs off. Valentine searches and at last drives to the judge's house, where she discovers that Rita has returned home. On this visit, Valentine also discovers that the judge uses sophisticated radio equipment to eavesdrop on his neighbours' telephone conversations. Valentine is repulsed, but the judge provokes her by posing difficult questions relating to the overheard conversations, and Valentine leaves, angry and confused.

Soon after, Valentine reads in a newspaper that the judge has been tried in court for his illegal eavesdropping. Valentine anxiously revisits the villa to assure the judge that she did not inform on him. The judge reveals that he had turned himself in because she had asked him to stop spying on his neighbours. By now, Rita has had pups, and Valentine and the judge continue their conversation, more receptive of each other's differences. As they talk, a window is smashed by a stone — another (the sixth) reminder of the offended neighbours' hostility.

Auguste's girlfriend, Karin, is one of the judge's neighbours, and when she attends the court proceedings against him, she meets a man. As a consequence, her relationship with Auguste breaks up, as the judge suspected it would, having eavesdropped on their conversations. But Auguste finds out the hard way. Karin does not return his calls, and he visits her apartment, where he climbs to a window and looks inside, discovering that his worst fears are true.

Valentine invites the judge to a fashion show where she is modelling. They talk after the show, and the judge reveals the event in his past that caused him to become embittered. He was betrayed by a woman he loved, and he did not recover. At this point we see that the judge's career and Auguste's have been replicas of one another. The film has given hints of this all along, but we now see that perhaps the young judge, Auguste, will meet Valentine, and realize the happiness that the old judge has forgone.

Valentine takes a ferry to England, to meet Michel. Auguste is on the same ferry, which capsizes in a storm. There are seven survivors — the three main couples from *Blue, White,* and *Red,* as well as an English barman. The judge watches a TV report on the survivors, and the camera focuses on Valentine and Auguste standing together, and then closes in on Valentine's profile, which duplicates the billboard photo. At the end, the judge looks at us through a broken pane of glass in his villa, his face expressing his complex emotions.

Red is beautiful to look at, and the photography of the interiors — especially the villa — is quietly seductive and intriguing. Repeatedly, shots are framed by doorways, partitions, mirrors, and windows, so that our point of view is limited or refracted and we don't see the whole picture. The light typically comes from shaded lamps and is often reflected or photographed through glass, lambent and producing complex patterns of shade and what Geoff Andrew calls a sense of "something immanent." Kieslowski thought carefully about these effects, and Irène Jacob describes how he would take a shot repeatedly to get the precise fall of light and shadow on her face. She did not know what Kieslowski was aiming at in each case, but she realized that the way light was photographed "would tell the story as well." For instance, in a scene where Valentine returns to the villa after the judge has turned himself in, they share tiny glasses of pear brandy, and they talk. A light bulb burns out, and the judge removes the shade and supplies a new bulb, which for a moment glares brightly. Valentine flinches and the judge replaces the shade, returning to the softer half-light in which he and Valentine continue their conversation. Darkness prevents their exchange, but the light cannot be too bright either. Just so, Valentine and the judge learn gradually from one another, as Valentine's initial moral certainty (too bright) is shaken, as is the judge's recalcitrant bitterness (too dark). The interplay of light and shade, the soft ambience, uncertain contours and multiple perspectives, represent the tentative rapprochement by which human beings (not just Valentine and the judge) make their way towards moral knowledge and mutual understanding, and this process is the core meaning of fraternity as *Red* presents it.

Irène Jacob says that Kieslowski had "a very precise idea of what he wanted," and Agnieszka Holland concurs that he was "extremely precise." "Very, very precise," adds Jean-Louis Trintignant, going on to explain how Kieslowski would insist that a head be turned so far and no further, or a glass placed exactly *here,* not there. *Red* is chock full of these kinds of precise details, which, however, are arranged and interwoven with such rhythmic eloquence that their deliberate construction is absorbed in the organic complexity of the film as a whole. But everywhere — as always in Kieslowski — the concrete particulars reveal the inner lives of people in whom we find ourselves interested, partly because we are affected by the power and implications of the "documentary" aspect of the film, despite the fact that we might not quite grasp how the details are working on us. Let us consider some examples.

As is quickly evident, Kieslowski uses the colour red everywhere. But there is no necessary connection between the colour and the central theme, fraternity. Rather, the significance of red is intrinsic to the film. Auguste's jeep, Valentine's sweater, the billboard, traffic lights, the outside trim of *Chez Joseph,* various pieces of furniture, a wrapper, a bowling ball, Michel's jacket, the dog's leash (as well as its blood) — all these, as well as countless other details, are red. Mainly, the colour provides continuity, interwoven throughout like the strands of Zbigniew Preisner's haunting bolero, which provides a beautiful musical enhancement to the pleasing visual orchestration of the colour as *leitmotif.* As Kieslowski says, in particular cases red is used for dramatic effect, but its meaning is not reducible to a single significance. Still, it is tempting to see a basic duality in the colour, corresponding, as it were, to the two interwoven strands that constitute the bolero. On the one hand, red suggests compassion, a warmth that emanates from Valentine and is especially associated with her by way of her red sweater and the billboard with her portrait against a red background. On the other hand, red suggests danger or alarm, as with Rita's blood (which gets onto Valentine's hands), the red traffic lights, and the lights of the surveillance vehicle which tracks the judge's illegal radio operation. Like a great many key images in the film, red is ambivalent, and its positive sense never stands quite clear from a trace of its negative opposite, and vice versa.

A similar ambivalence is evident in the way Kieslowski deals with glass (windows, mirrors, drinking glasses), telephones, dogs, coins, and breath (or wind), as well as the intricate parallels between the judge and Auguste, signalled by pens, car batteries, dogs, books, and the (fictional) composer Van den Budenmayer. There is too much here to describe in detail, but let us briefly consider breath, and how Kieslowski shows that the generous, warm-hearted, and vulnerable Valentine is, as it were, a breath of life for the embittered, reclusive judge.

Early in the film, Valentine shoots a chewing-gum ad. Jacques, the photographer, asks her to blow a bubble with the gum, and explains that the ad will display the motto "Breath of Life." But neither this photo nor the motto is used in the final version of the ad which appears on the giant billboard. The ad is printed on fabric attached to a wooden frame, and shows Valentine in profile against a lustrous red background. In the top left corner we might catch the words "en toute circonstance fraîcheur de vivre" ("in every situation the freshness of living"). A viewer has to look carefully and the message is easy to miss (more on this later).

Clearly, considerable care has gone into this sequence of shots. The image of Valentine blowing the bubble represents and confirms the idea that she is an agent of what Jacques calls "The Breath of Life." The haunting beauty of the ad itself would be lost if it showed the pink bubble of gum, but the idea of Valentine's freshness and vitality is maintained by the words on the top left. Interestingly, the ad is situated at the intersection where Valentine runs over Rita, and where, later, both Auguste and the judge pause at a red light and are absorbed by her picture until impatient motorists honk and move them on.

The breath of life we now associate with Valentine recurs in the form of a spring breeze, which on two occasions stirs the dead leaves in front of the judge's villa when Valentine visits. The significance of the stirring leaves is confirmed by the exchange between Valentine and the judge in which she responds to his bitter declaration that he wants nothing from life. "Then stop breathing," she says, as the judge goes into the house to look for change he owes her for the vet bill. As Valentine waits, the wind blows the leaves into a little flurry, and when the judge fails to return, Valentine becomes impatient and calls out, "Are you not breathing any more?" She then follows him into the house, as he intended, where she discovers his illegal eavesdropping.

The contrast between Valentine's life-giving energy and the judge's bitter negativity is registered by the stirring breeze and the dead leaves, and also by the verbal exchange about breathing. Yet Kieslowski does not present us with a simple contrast. We recall that the breeze later turns into a storm, and Valentine's ad is hastily taken down as the breath of life turns into a tempest that sinks the ferry. At the rescue scene, the final shot of Valentine's profile against a red background duplicates the ad. She has not drowned. She lives and breathes, and, like the judge, she has a second chance.

For his part, the judge watches the report of the accident on TV and then looks at us through a broken window. His expression is a mixture of relief, gratitude, and sadness. Some commentators (Insdort, Kickasola) say that tears run down his face, matching the tearful faces at the end of *Blue* and *White*. By contrast, Geoff Andrew says that the judge smiles. For the life of me, I can't see the tears, but also, the smile is so faint as to be almost vestigial. As I see it, the judge's expression is a mixture of wistfulness, relief, gratitude, pained resignation. He is a sadder and a wiser man, and the highly talented Jean-Louis Trintignant catches the richly ambivalent beauty of what I take to be Kieslowski's conception of the judge's state of mind. The judge knows that Valentine is safe. She has been his breath of life, humanizing him, and the glass behind which he withdrew into isolation is broken. But also the judge knows his loss. Valentine and he might have been happy together had she been a generation younger, but now the young judge, Auguste, will take the old judge's place. We recall also that the glass is broken by the judge's resentful neighbours — a reminder of his alienation and of happiness foregone, lost to bitterness.

As elsewhere in *Red,* broken glass (and the spillage of the liquids glasses contain) suggests loss of communion, failure of communication, and pain of separation. And so the judge experiences happiness and grief indissolubly mixed. As with the ambivalence of glass and the breath-wind-storm motif, his final, direct gaze at us does not let us come to rest comfortably on a simple conclusion. "It's a harsh film," says Irène Jacob, and for all its beauty and compassion, *Red* is unflinching in how it deals with pain, imperfection, and grief.

Kieslowski believed that suffering is ineradicable, and although we struggle for freedom we are largely unfree. "I believe we are just as much prisoners of our own passions, our own physiology, and certainly our own biology, as we were thousands of years ago." "We're always trying to find a way out. But we're constantly imprisoned by our passions and feelings" (150). Yet in itself the impulse to find a way out contradicts the determinism, and Kieslowski was convinced from an early age (especially, he says, as a result of reading books) that "there was something more to life than material things" (5). Later, he admits that "certain religious questions" arise in his work, and "what I'm thinking of is caring also for the audience's spiritual life. Maybe that's too strong a word but something which is a little more than just box office" (209). Kieslowski pulls back here from the word "spiritual" even as he uses it, and his films never offer religious solutions to moral problems. Still, he remains sensitive to the aspirations, anxieties, and desire for liberation and communion that move people towards religion, and his films frequently raise questions about the mystery of existence, the meaning of life, freedom, memory, destiny — questions that religion offers to answer, but Kieslowski does not.

As we see, Kieslowski evokes the metaphysical mainly by way of concrete details: chance encounters, coincidences, repeated patterns of various kinds. And here we might notice a central, thematic counterpoise between his conviction that we are controlled by the mechanisms of our physical bodies and the fact that our struggle for freedom is pervaded by a mystery which is irreducible to its material antecedents. In *Red,* this counterpoise is represented especially by Kieslowski's treatment of dogs, on the one hand, and chance, coincidence, and memory, on the other.

Rita (and her pups) play a key role in *Red.* Kieslowski acknowledges this, explaining how difficult it was to film the dog, which, for instance, was required to look back and forth between Valentine and the judge when Valentine returns to the villa after Rita runs home. "We wanted the dog to be the catalyst," Kieslowski says, "that would bring our two heroes together." Also, this is "the first critical moment in the movie" because from this point everything changes, as Valentine connects with the judge. The dog is therefore pivotal, representing a connectedness based on sense and feeling rather than opinions and ideas. Throughout *Red,* kindness to animals is life-affirming, and neglect or cruelty is the opposite. Thus, the judge develops an affection for Rita and her pups, in contrast to his initial, emotionally sterile indifference. Auguste also has a dog, which romps boisterously. But when Auguste is betrayed by Karin, he returns to his apartment and lashes out angrily as the animal greets him, so that the dog yelps in pain and alarm. The distracted Auguste then abandons the dog, which he ties to a post on a busy road before driving off. But when we see him on the ferry, he is reunited with his dog, which he carries in his arms, and we see that he has relented and bitterness has not prevailed. Finally, the fact that Rita has seven pups, corresponding to the seven survivors of the disaster, suggests that animal life is the gift of life itself, and calls for affirmation.

"Breath of life" is the root meaning of "spirit," but, Kieslowski insists, spirit needs to be embodied, and we are not human without being physical, passionate, alive in the senses. Valentine, whose character would be easy to idealize and who talks a good deal about moral issues, also needs the physical dimension. That is why Kieslowski shows (twice) her ballet class, in which she sweats, holding prolonged stretches that make her grunt and gasp. After the first class, we watch her guzzle a bottle of water, hardly able to pour it down fast enough.

Interestingly, in the background of this shot — across the street — is a church, which turns out to be the church into which Rita bolts when she runs away. Valentine follows Rita inside, where Mass is being celebrated, and she is uncomfortably aware of interrupting the religious ceremony, even as she wants to know where Rita is. In an interview, Kieslowski remarks on how deliberate is this pairing of the two shots of the church, even though many viewers might not pick up on it. I will return to this point by and by; meanwhile, the scene with the dog in the church suggests the interweaving of body and spirit, confirming what is implied by the fact that Valentine's greedy drinking is framed by the church in the background. And so at last, in counterpoint to the moral intensity of their conversations,

Valentine also teaches the judge that he needs the warmth of a life-affirming affection, and, in turn, he has to acknowledge that the physical relationship that Valentine needs (to slake her thirst, as it were) will be provided by the young judge, and not by the old one.

If the dogs tell us about the body's natural affections, Kieslowski's use of coincidence, chance, and patterned repetition opens upon a non-rational sense of the mystery that emerges from people's ability to reflect on the sheer strangeness of existence. Chance encounters, missed phone calls, tossed coins, the slot machine in *Chez Joseph* (we recall that the Judge's name is also Joseph), repeated or parallel motifs (for instance, two pens, two books falling open at a key page, two batteries running down) — such things gather and fill, and their accumulated weight, as well as their unemphatic integration into the story, get us wondering about relationships between chance and freedom, meaning and contingency, memory and time.

Kieslowski says that the repetition of motifs in *Red* encourages audiences "to think retrospectively" and to recognize or remember things they had seen earlier. As an example, he discusses the shot of the church to which the dog runs, and on which he deliberately caused the camera to linger in order to provide a hint to the audience that they had seen this church before — in the background as Valentine was drinking water after the ballet class. It would be easy to miss this detail, and Kieslowski then adds, disconcertingly, "of course it's not important" (6). But what is important, he goes on to say, is that he "tried to accumulate these signs" in the expectation that members of an audience would get some of them — enough to cause individual viewers to suspect that such effects are worked all through the film and that there are more such effects than the ones consciously detected. Kieslowski says that memory works in just that way — imperfectly and intermittently — and images can be stored in the unconscious (6), so that we can have intuitions, inclinations, suspicions, emotional responses, premonitions, and the like, which emerge from dimensions of experience we have forgotten but which remain, as it were, in the pre-articulate recesses of the body itself. By such means, Kieslowski gives us a view of the world simultaneously concrete and metaphysical, material and mysterious.

As we see, the dogs in *Red* confront us with the immediacy of physical life and its reproduction, and the main characters are implicitly judged by how they treat the animals. But dogs do not think about justice, morality, love, pain, memory, the meaning of life, and the mystery of existence. People do that, but not without being captive also to the passions of the body, their own animal life, the compulsions of biology which are far more complex than ideas. People struggle for a freedom they do not have, for justice that remains unattainable, for love which remains imperfect. The best things that they do for one another emerge from an acceptance of this struggle, and of each other's imperfect understandings, individual differences, and personal insecurities. These are the beginnings of what fraternity — the topic of *Red* — might mean. As Zbigniew Preisner says, *Red* is a film against indifference, and certainly it is a film about compassion. But it is not sentimental or soft-centred. Fraternity is incompatible with acquiescence to injustice, and is forged in the teeth of tragedy and pain. Although Kieslowski says he eschewed politics, as Slavoj Žižek says (*The Fright of Real Tears* [London: British Film Institute, 2001]), the "highest reconciliation" is that of the "fraternity" (164) which remakes the community itself, and such a thing occurs in *Three Colours* only in *Red,* which Kieslowski himself thought the summation of his career.

In an interesting reflection, Kieslowski acknowledges that it is a beautiful thing to be able to give of ourselves, as, for instance, Valentine does. But he then raises the question (posed also to Valentine by the judge) of whether or not self-giving is prompted by the fact that "we want to have a better opinion of ourselves." Kieslowski says we can never know the answer: "Is this beauty pure? Or is it always a little marred? That's the question the film asks" (218).

I want to suggest that, yes, the beauty is "a little marred," but this is what makes it beautiful. Kieslowski has said that he never achieved what he wanted in a film; the result always fell short. Yet, as the cinematographer, Piotr Sobocinski, says, Kieslowski "always asks you to go as deep as possible, past your limits, and this is beautiful." The achievement therefore does not lie in some perfect realization, but in the way in which the ideal is sought in spite of imperfection, and with courage, compassion, imagination, and a willingness to go further than you can, even if you know you cannot go far enough. The fraternity of those proceeding in such a spirit is a central value I have sought to affirm in the preceding chapters — a value that can be represented and summarized by Kieslowski's complex understanding of the imperfections that remain always a condition of our histori-cally situated, human solidarity.

Bibliographical Notes

I have kept the notes to a minimum, partly by incorporating bibliographical data in the body of the writing. Where possible, I use editions that are likely to be most accessible to readers.

Chapter 1

References are to *Plato, The Republic,* trans. H.D.P. Lee (Harmondsworth: Penguin, 1964).

Chapter 2

References are to *Vincent Van Gogh — The Letters*, ed. Leo Jansen, Hans Luijten, and Nienke Bakker, 6 vols. (New York: Thames and Hudson, 2009). Letter numbers are indicated in the text. The complete letters, in fully searchable form, are available at http://vangoghletters.org/vg/.

Chapter 3

References are to *Julian of Norwich, Showings,* trans. from the critical text by Edmund Colledge, O.S.A., and James Walsh, S.J. (New York: Paulist Press, 1978).

Chapter 4

References are to *The Mahavamsa, or The Great Chronicle of Ceylon,* trans. Wilhelm Geiger (London: Oxford University Press, 1912).

Chapter 6

References are to the *Majjima Nikaya* (Middle Length Discourses), *Digha Nikaya* (Long Discourses), and *Samyutta Nikaya* (Connected Discourses). I refer to these as MD, LD, and CD. Page numbers for MD refer to *The Middle Length Discourses of the Buddha,* trans. Bhikkhu Nanamoli (Boston: Wisdom Publications, 1995); for LD, *The Long Discourses of the Buddha,* trans. Maurice Walshe (Boston: Wisdom Publications, 1995), and for CD, *The Connected Discourses of the Buddha,* trans. Bhikkhu Bodhi (Boston: Wisdom Publications, 2000).

Chapter 9

References are to *The Comedy of Dante Alighieri,* trans. Dorothy L. Sayers and Barbara Reynolds (Harmondsworth: Penguin, 1962); *John Donne, The Elegies and the Songs and Sonnets,* ed. Helen Gardner (Oxford: Clarendon Press, 1965); and Samuel Beckett, *Murphy* (1938; New York: Grove Press, 1970).

Chapter 10 and Chapter 16

Quotations from *Henry V* and *Romeo and Juliet* are from *The Complete Signet Classic Shakespeare* (New York: Harcourt, Brace, Jovanovich, 1972).

Chapter 13

References are to Lao Tsu, *Tao Te Ching,* trans. Gia-Fu Feng and Jane English (New York: Vintage, 1989); *The Book of Chuang Tzu,* trans. Martin Palmer (London: Arkana, 1996); and *Lieh-Tzu: A Taoist Guide to Practical Living,* trans. Eva Wong (Boston: Shambhala, 1995).

Chapter 15

References are to *The Book of Psalms,* trans. Robert Alter (New York: Norton, 2007).

Chapter 17

References are to *The Meaning of the Holy Qur'an,* trans. 'Abdullah Yūsuf 'Alī, 11th ed., with rev. English translation, commentary and index (Beltsville, MD: Amana Publications, 2006).

Chapter 18

References are to *The Aeneid,* trans. Frank O. Copley (New York: Bobbs-Merrill, 1965).

Chapter 19

References are to Ananda Guruge, ed., *Return to Righteousness: A Collection of Speeches, Essays and Letters of the Anagarika Dharmapala* (Ceylon: Government Press, 1965).

Chapter 20

References are to *The Essential Jung,* ed. Anthony Storr (Princeton, NJ: Princeton University Press, 1983), and to *The Collected Works of C.G. Jung,* ed. H. Read, M. Fordham, and G. Adler, trans. R.F.C. Hull (London: Routledge, and Princeton, NJ: Princeton University Press, 1961–83), referred to in the text as *CW* and cited by volume and paragraph number, in accordance with convention. I have used an accessible edition of *The Secret of the Golden Flower* (New York: Harcourt Brace, 1962).

Chapter 21

References are to the remarkably comprehensive interviews with Kieslowski, edited by Danusia Stok, *Kieslowski on Kieslowski* (London: Faber, 1993). Other quotations are drawn from interviews supplied as additional material on the CD *Three Colours.*